The New
Secrets
of
Style

INSTYLE

EDITORIAL
Managing Editor Ariel Foxman
Creative Director Rina Stone
Deputy Managing Editor Lisa Arbetter
Executive Editor Leonora Wiener
Assistant Managing Editor Patrick Moffitt
Director of Photography Marie Suter
Deputy Editors Donna Bulseco, Nancy Bilyeau
Editorial Operations Director Lavinel Savu

Fashion Directors Hal Rubenstein,
Cynthia Weber Cleary
Market Director Erin Sumwalt
Accessories Director Meggan Crum
Fashion Features Editor Megan Deem
Senior Style Editor Sydne Bolden Long
Senior Market Editor Samantha Bishopp Mollett
Market Editor Dana Avidan
Assistant Accessories Editor Sabrina Strelitz

Copy Chief Marcia Lawther
Deputy Copy Chief Sandra Vernet

Chief of Reporters DeLora E. Jones
Deputy Chief of Reporters Subira Shaw

Associate Production Manager Bijal Saraiya

Imaging Manager Steven Cadicamo

Executive Director, Public Relations Beth A. Mitchell

Instyle.com Editor Rosie Amodio

PUBLISHING
Publisher Connie Anne Phillips
Vice President, Finance Maria Tucci Beckett
Vice President, Consumer Marketing Holley Cavanna
Consumer Marketing Directors Stephanie Chan,
Dana Kappel

Legal Nicholas J. Jollymore, Esq., Helen Wan, Esq.

THE NEW SECRETS OF STYLE
Editor Isabel González Whitaker
Special Projects Editor Robin Sayers
Copy Editor Kim Tingley
Reporter Qimmah Saafir
Editorial Assistant Elisabeth Durkin

TIME INC. HOME ENTERTAINMENT
Publisher Richard Fraiman
General Manager Steven Sandonato
Executive Director, Marketing Services Carol Pittard
Director, Retail & Special Sales Tom Mifsud
Director, New Product Development Peter Harper
Assistant Director, Bookazine Marketing Laura Adam
Assistant Publishing Director,
Brand Marketing Joy Butts
Associate Manager, Product Marketing Nina Fleishman
Design & Prepress Manager Anne-Michelle Gallero
Book Production Manager Susan Chodakiewicz

Time Inc. Home Entertainment would also like to
thank: Christine Austin, Glenn Buonocore, Jim Childs,
Rose Cirrincione, Jacqueline Fitzgerald, Lauren Hall,
Jennifer Jacobs, Suzanne Janso, Brynn Joyce, Mona Li,
Robert Marasco, Amy Migliaccio, Brooke Reger,
Dave Rozzelle, Ilene Schreider, Adriana Tierno,
Alex Voznesenskiy, Sydney Webber

MELCHER MEDIA
This book was produced by Melcher Media, Inc.
124 West 13th St.
New York, NY 10011
www.melcher.com

Publisher Charles Melcher
Associate Publisher Bonnie Eldon
Editor in Chief Duncan Bock

Executive Editor Lia Ronnen
Project Editor Lauren Nathan
Editorial Assistant Coco Joly
Production Director Kurt Andrews
Production Assistant Daniel del Valle

Photo Researcher Sierra Fromberg
Copy Editor Heidi Ernst

The New Secrets of Style

Your complete guide to dressing your best every day by the editors of *InStyle*

Written by Jennifer Alfano
Designed by Bess Yoham

PRODUCED BY MELCHER MEDIA FOR *INSTYLE* AND TIME INC. HOME ENTERTAINMENT

contents

foreword

As we wrote when we published the original *Secrets of Style*, the first thing to realize is that this is not a fashion book. Books, after all, are permanent—or as permanent as something printed on paper can be. Fashion, by its very definition, is constantly changing.

Style, however, is something else altogether, a distinctive way you speak, act or dress. While there's no doubt that style, or stylishness, comes easier to some than to others, we still believe—make that, insist—that every woman can develop great personal style. It's just a matter of determining what works best for you. And that's where we come in.

Some readers of this book may be familiar with *InStyle*, but many of you may not. For 15 years we've been covering the stylish lives of celebrities—especially the choices they make when it comes to beauty and fashion. In editing the magazine and Web site, we've worked with and interviewed the top style-makers who help these stars look their best, in front of the cameras and offscreen.

Since we began, *InStyle*'s fashion coverage has grown under the talented hands and knowing eyes of our fashion directors, Hal Rubenstein and Cindy Weber Cleary, and their team. Even with all the changes in the celebrity and fashion worlds—with the immediate and constant access to style information of every sort—their mission has remained steadfast: to make fashion understandable, achievable and, maybe most importantly, fun. Their ability to articulate the vision of *InStyle*'s founding editor, Martha Nelson—that the magazine talks to the reader as a trusted friend—is evident every month, and now in the updated version of this book: Advising, not dictating, encouraging instead of admonishing, and, above all, being a reality-based style adviser, it cheers on readers to embrace all the positive things fashion can do for them.

While many of us wouldn't mind looking like one of today's top stars (Jennifer Aniston, Beyoncé or Reese Witherspoon, to name just a few)—women we cover every month in *InStyle*—the truth of the matter is that we don't. We're taller or shorter. Our figures are bustier or more boyish. Our lives and lifestyles are not the same. What we can do is learn from their successes (or mistakes). We can analyze what works and what doesn't and develop a personal style that is right for each of us.

We hope *The New Secrets of Style* will help you do just that. We've gathered the very latest information about fit, from pants to jackets to bras to bathing suits; clarified the right cuts for a particular figure; culled the best advice about flattering

tones and colors; and provided smart shopping strategies to try both in-store and online. While a book's worth of information may seem like an awful lot of thought to give to clothing (no matter how difficult finding the right pieces may be), the idea is that if you do a bit of thinking up front, your life will be a lot easier on a daily basis. After reading through these pages, we hope you'll have a wardrobe that coordinates easily, fills your needs, flatters your figure and fits your body. And that you'll know which looks from a season's trend offerings will work best with what you already own. Or put another way, we hope you'll never again stand in front of a packed closet and say, "I've got nothing to wear!"

But perhaps the most important thing this book can give you is the confidence to pursue the style that works best for you. Ultimately, we hope we can help you to look—and feel—your best every day!

ARIEL FOXMAN
Managing Editor, InStyle

STYLE

chapter 1

Fundamentals

"Fashions fade. Style is eternal."

These five simple words from designer Yves Saint Laurent sum up the philosophy of this book—because trends come and trends go, but being stylish has real staying power.

We're endlessly inspired by the seemingly effortless glamour of Hollywood, but there's usually a small army of experts working behind the scenes to help stars achieve their red-carpet victories. What to do if your only consultant when dressing is your trusty mirror?

The quest to nail down your personal style is like driving: Sometimes you know exactly where you're going, but other times you get totally lost along the way (owing to reasons that run the gamut from shifting gears into a new phase of life to simply a closet in need of a tune-up). Whatever the cause of your fashion flat tire, style fundamentals can come to your rescue— knowing what works best for you, regardless of the hot color or hem length of any given season. Fundamentals are like a GPS for your look, always steering you in a fashionable direction.

SARAH JESSICA PARKER's sense of style rivals even that of alter ego Carrie Bradshaw's. Here, a simple cardigan over a sleek sheath conveys classic sophistication.

RACHEL BILSON nails casual chic in a go-to look for all ages: a fitted blazer over a basic button-front paired with crisp wide-leg jeans. Her boyish belt is the perfect final touch.

Proving she knows what works on her, singer ALICIA KEYS creates balance between her top and bottom by baring her arms. The waist-cinching detail plays up her sexy shape.

Ankle boots and a motor-cycle jacket on GWYNETH PALTROW say bold and edgy. It's not all tough, though: The minidress and leg-lengthening tights project feminine appeal.

find your look

Determining whether you're a minimalist (less is more) or a romantic (more is more) or something in between is the crucial first step on the road to fashion satisfaction.

T he key to looking fabulous begins with identifying what kind of style personality you have. Then you need to narrow in on those wardrobe items that are right for you. The good news is that decoding your look not only yields rewards in the long run, it brings instant gratification because it's fun. Really!

Here's how to start: Set aside a weekend afternoon. Gather up all your favorite magazines, then rip out pages featuring awe-inspiring looks or tastemakers (women who, to you, epitomize great style). Skip red-carpet gowns and cocktail dresses, and stick to everyday pieces and looks.

Next, make an itemized list of a dozen of your absolute favorite pieces of clothing and accessories that you own. Study both this list and those magazine clippings, then ask yourself some questions: Are you a casual type who prefers jeans and jackets with flats? Or perhaps you have a bohemian bent and live for flowing peasant shirts, long skirts and boots? Or do you just die for anything romantic, such as sherbet shades, ruffles and chiffon? Do you find yourself favoring trends or perennial classics such as pencil skirts, cardigans and pumps? Are you someone who loves tailored pieces for work but easygoing looks on the weekend?

The important thing here is to be honest with yourself and concentrate on the looks you like most. Write down your preferences to help define your style succinctly (for example, ladylike luxe or laid-back hippie chic). Now comes the hard part: sticking to this defined style. Edit out closet dwellers that don't fit the criteria. Anything borderline gets cut, including those pieces you only feel brave enough to wear once in a while. Pieces that aren't totally flattering? Gone too. Why so harsh? Because women who have become icons of timeless, impeccable style all had the ability to know what worked for them and what made them feel good, and they stuck to their formula no matter what. Following such fantastic examples teaches us to be more disciplined about how we dress day in and day out.

MINKA KELLY shows us her refined, classic style in a pencil skirt and ruffled blouse.

JOY BRYANT expresses her eclectic tendencies in layers and untraditional pairings.

style basics

Dressing your best involves more than just knowing what you like. Here, the three vital criteria for finding a garment that's a keeper.

KATE MOSS lengthens her legs by wearing a cropped jacket over a sheath.

Fit

Good fit means that clothes skim the body (showing curves without clinging to them), and that all the details—lapels, pocket flaps, slits, seams and pleats—lie flat. Whenever clothing pulls or buckles, it not only looks sloppy, it also adds pounds. The same holds true for garments that are too big. In the following chapters, you'll learn what a tailor can do for you and that even the small stuff—such as adjusting a skirt hem, the length of a jacket, or the width of a sleeve—can make a huge difference in your overall appearance.

Fabric

The two most important qualities to look for in fabric are weight and movement. If a fabric is too stiff, it can look boxy; too thin, and it may cling to every bulge; too shiny, and it can add pounds. Fabrics such as wool crêpe, wool microfiber blends, cotton or wool gabardine, cotton blended with silk and some synthetics are generally good choices. A touch of spandex helps too (3 to 5 percent is usually plenty).

Keep in mind that matte fabrics are more forgiving than shiny ones. Contrasting fabric textures (such as tweed and silk) also add visual interest to an outfit.

Proportion

Of course, everything can fit properly, but if you don't get the proportions right, you will still be off the mark. Flattering your figure is not just about camouflage and diversion—it's also a balancing act. The length of your legs in relation to your torso, the width of your shoulders in relation to your hips: These things matter. Luckily, such details are a cinch to manipulate visually to your advantage.

Head-to-Toe Slenderizing Tricks

One of the most flattering tricks for using proportion to your advantage is to choose looks that are either "short over long" or "long over short." For example, a cropped jacket over a knee-length shift will give your waist definition while also providing the illusion of lengthening your bottom half. Conversely, a long jacket with skinny pants or a tunic over a shorter pencil skirt that hits above or at the knee creates a long-over-short outfit with a top-to-bottom slimming effect.

BEYONCE finds an ideal fit in a wrap-style dress that makes the most of her figure.

flatter your figure

Once you know your style, find clothes that accentuate your physique.

Shape	Goal	Look for	Avoid
Curvy	Defining your waist, elongating your figure and showing off your curves without overemphasizing them.	• Pieces that fall smoothly over your curves. • Dresses and skirts that are nipped in at the waist. • Monochromatic separates.	• Anything oversize or too tight. • Very thin fabrics. • Clothes lacking seams, like bust and waist darts, to follow your figure. • Long jackets and those that button loosely at the waist. • Tops and jackets that end at the fullest part of your hips.
Short	Elongating your legs and creating a strong vertical line from head to toe.	• Monochromatic outfits. • Fluid fabrics. • Empire-waist tops and dresses. • Vertical lines.	• Stiffly tailored clothes. • Horizontal prints. • Pleated trousers. • Midcalf-length and full, pleated skirts. • Anything baggy or voluminous.
Narrow Shoulders	Squaring your shoulders and creating balance between them and your hips.	• Jackets with light padding or shoulder detail. • Tops with horizontal lines or patterns. • Boatneck tops or those with a wide V-neck.	• Raglan sleeves (with seams running diagonally from under the arms toward the neck). • Body-hugging T-shirts.
Broad Shoulders	Softening your shoulders.	• Soft, feminine blouses. • Cardigan sweaters in place of jackets. • For those with slim hips, bottoms with horizontal patterns for balance.	• Epaulets. • Shoulder pads. • Horizontal lines at the shoulders, including seams and wide lapels. • Boatneck tops. • Sleeveless or cap-sleeve tops.
Full Bust	Showing your curves without overemphasizing them and elongating your torso and neck.	• Simple tops. • Open-neck, wrap, and V-neck tops and dresses. • Anything that adds a vertical line above the waist.	• Double-breasted styles. • Wide belts. • Collars with large lapels. • Puffy sleeves. • Tops or jackets made from stiff fabrics. • Baggy tops.

Shape	Goal	Look for	Avoid
Small Bust	Showcasing the curves you've got.	• Belts to accent your waist. • Fitted tops and jackets. • Body-hugging T-shirts. • Slim-cut sleeveless shifts and tops. • Tops with draping and shirring bust details.	• Wrap dresses and tops. • Loose or overly structured tops. • Tops made out of stiff fabrics. • Very low-cut tops.
Heavy Arms	Slimming and elongating your arms and torso.	• Long-sleeve tops or those that end just below the elbow. • Raglan, dolman and kimono sleeves. • V-necks.	• Tight tops and sleeves. • Tops made out of stiff fabrics. • Tops with puffy sleeves.
Tummy	Refocusing attention from your middle to your legs or face and creating one long vertical line.	• Long tops such as tunics, cardigans and jackets. • Empire-waist tops and dresses. • A-line shifts that skim the body.	• Belted dresses and tops. • Belts in bright colors or with lots of flourishes like embroidery or metal studs. • Tops with waistbands or anything that cinches. • Pants or skirts with waist detailing.

Short or Long Waist?

Do you have a short waist (short torso, longer legs) or a long waist (long torso, shorter legs)? Measure the distance between your bottom rib and the top of your hip bone. If it's just a few inches, you have a short waist; 4 or more inches, and you have a long waist. Once you know, you'll want to wear a waistband that balances your top and bottom halves. If you have a short waist, look for lower waistlines, and if you have a long waist, look for higher ones.

fabrics, patterns and details

Having a working knowledge of fabric types and finishes takes much of the mystery out of shopping and helps you gravitate toward those looks that flatter you most.

Wool

Wool comes in various weights and weaves. The heaviest, including boiled and felted versions, are perfect for winter coats because they are warm, durable and don't wrinkle. Medium-weight wools—menswear suiting, tweed and flannel—hold the structure of a jacket and can be cut into tailored skirts and trousers. Lightweight wools—gabardines, tropical-worsted pieces and jerseys—are good for multi-seasonal garments that are often softer in shape.

Cotton

Like wool, cotton is versatile. Thick, tight weaves work for denim, suiting and warm-weather coats. Crisp piqués, chambrays, poplins and broadcloths are best for button-front shirts and summer-weight dresses. Voiles and softer, thinner weights make nice sheer blouses and billowy skirts and dresses. Then there is cotton T-shirt material, often with a bit of Lycra.

Cashmere

Cashmere is known for its breathability, softness and warmth. The key factors in determining its quality are where the fibers are from and where those fibers are woven into the fabric. The best fibers usually come from Mongolia or China, while the top mills (where the cashmere is processed and knitted) tend to be located in Italy and Scotland. Cashmere also comes in several plies—from single, used in light pieces such as scarves, to 10, found in thick-knit sweaters and other garments.

Silk

Silks range from floaty, sheer chiffon to raw douppioni and shantung. Of course, all silk is not created equal: A good, classic silk weave should drape beautifully, fall softly and lay lightly in your hand when held, while cheap silk tends to be overly shiny and stiff.

Synthetic

Microfibers and other manufactured fabrics such as Tencel are popping up both on runways and at your local discount superstore. Mixing classic wools, cashmeres and cottons with hints of Lycra helps fabrics hold their shape and fit better. Rayon and viscose blends create fluid, easy-to-care-for clothes that flatter most bodies and are ideal for travel.

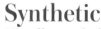

Patterns

With patterns, think about color and size. Know that tonal patterns (pink on red, say) attract less attention, and that the darker the background, the more slimming the design.

As for size, always choose patterns according to your proportions. Tiny, low-contrast prints are flattering for petite figures, while taller women can often pull off bigger patterns that have more contrast.

Looking for a pattern that slims? Bigger prints work, but only in low-contrast designs or diagonal patterns. If you are choosing stripes, vertical lines are preferable to horizontal ones, and diagonal lines that are more vertical than horizontal will also have an elongating effect.

Details and Flourish

Details can be used to draw attention to a part of your body you want to emphasize. The ruffled neckline of a blouse can show off your décolleté, or the straps of a low-back dress can emphasize the toning benefits of all those Pilates classes.

A word of caution, however: Excessive detailing can create a questionable overall look, date your clothes, minimize an outfit's versatility, and make you look heavier. Anything that adds an additional layer or girth—ruffles, patch pockets, wide lapels, big buttons or epaulets—accentuates what's underneath. For instance, a safari jacket complete with pockets and a belt might be high on style, but a simpler, less-detailed top could be the more slimming option. Choose your details wisely, and limit yourself to just one stunning eye-catcher.

Fabrics: A Primer

The adage "You get what you pay for" is gospel with fabric. Cheap fabrics tend to be less flattering, while higher-quality fabrics look better, last longer and hold their shape. Most fabrics fall into two categories: knitted or woven. Knits are best suited for body-contouring styles. Woven fabrics are stronger and hold form better, but because they are less flexible than knits, they might need a lot of tailoring for a perfect fit. Tightly woven fabrics (like denim) are preferable for heartier, semifitted fare, while less tightly woven fabrics (such as chiffon) are better for loose-fitting, gathered garments.

This pattern keeps the eye from settling on any one aspect of THANDIE NEWTON's figure.

choose your colors

Ever have one of those days when everyone comments on how radiant you look? Chances are you've hit upon a flattering color. The right one can do wonders, brightening your eyes and evening out your skin tone. The wrong choice will have you reaching for more makeup.

Everyone can wear every color—it all comes down to finding the right shade of that color for you. The shades that suit you depend on your skin tone as well as the color of your hair and eyes. Some general—but certainly not written-in-stone—guidelines are as follows: Women with pale skin and dark hair (the darkest browns and black) and women with blond hair often do well with saturated brights such as violet, red, royal blue and emerald green. Women with medium-brown to dark-blond hair and warmer, darker skin tones often do better with tempered alternatives such as lavender, coral, turquoise and olive green. Of course, someone with jet-black hair and pale skin can also look good in olive green, but it might be the emerald shade that really makes her stand out in a crowd.

Experiment with lots of different colors, always examining yourself in daylight against a white background. (Remember, artificial lighting and the presence of other colors change a color's tone.) If you're trying on a piece in a store without windows, take it home, but check the store's return policy first. As a rule, imperfections are more noticeable on light-colored fabric and less so on darker materials.

You'll likely find many wearable colors—but, in the interest of a working closet, you'll be better off limiting your wardrobe to a few neutrals (such as beige, black and white), and three or four bright colors that coordinate with them for each season. And don't be afraid to try a colored skirt with a top in a different hue, or one pastel paired with something more shocking. Being brave with color can be totally liberating!

This sunshine yellow complements LINDSAY PRICE's dark hair and eyes.

A print in an explosion of pink flatters CAMILLA BELLE's olive skin tone.

DEBRA MESSING's jewel-toned green dress and rich red hair look luxe, not holiday.

Going Monochrome

There are compelling reasons to dress in one color. A long, unbroken color line creates a polished look and makes you appear slimmer. Stark color-contrasts form horizontal lines that divide your body, sometimes making it appear wider and shorter.

Dark shades are the most slimming, but that doesn't mean you should rule out bright color. Color is an elixir, and if a deep amethyst dress or a pale lemon silk shirt paired with a yellow tweed skirt makes you feel feminine and confident, by all means, take advantage.

Wearing Light and Bright

Light and bright colors can draw attention to the parts of your figure that you want to accentuate. While dark colors might make you look slimmer, lighter shades can brighten your face, lift your mood and showcase your individuality.

You should never be afraid of color, but there are ways to overdo it. A good general rule—with the exception of prints—is to stick to a maximum of three colors in any given outfit. Any more, and the colors lose their punch.

You can also use color strategically. Combining brights with darks helps to balance your silhouette. (Darks minimize; lights highlight.) If you prefer to stick with darker shades, you can accent your look with a pair of bright heels, a bag in a bold hue, or a vibrant statement necklace.

Always edgy, SIENNA MILLER opts for a graphic treatment of red, gold and black.

Subtle pastels can look soft on fair skin, as demonstrated by EMMY ROSSUM.

KERRY WASHINGTON's vivid yellow long-sleeve top can't help but draw attention up.

play with color

Always reaching for the "safe" neutrals in your closet? While you're in the midst of giving your wardrobe a reboot, add a new hue to your basic tones. There's no need to worry about going overboard—you can adjust any hue's intensity to suit your mood.

Update Navy and White

YOU NOW HAVE:

MIX IT UP WITH:

Nautical, crisp and clean, this graphic color-duo is loved by traditionalists and minimalists. Add fun by going for saturated brights such as purple, kelly green, bright yellow and even fuchsia.

Perk Up Shades of Gray

YOU NOW HAVE:

MIX IT UP WITH:

Pale, muted neutrals worn from head to toe can look flat or cold, but if you throw in some tonal pastels—lavender, peach, sky blue and blush—you'll end up with a sophisticated, anything-but-dull alternative.

Patterned heels and a big mustard-hued bag add edge to MILLA JOVOVICH's otherwise preppy navy-and-white-striped dress.

This gray clutch mixes nicely with the peachy shades in CLAIRE DANES's dress.

Beyond Khaki and Olive

YOU NOW HAVE:

MIX IT UP WITH:

Sure, they fit with your earthy vibe, but you can overdose on these two shades. To add a spark, mix in standout fabrics, such as silks or satins, in spicy hues, such as pumpkin, saffron and wine.

Olive hues are far from blah when the fabric is shiny and formfitting, as seen on JESSICA BIEL.

beyond the basics

Now that you have a solid foundation laid out, there are still a few key pieces of style advice that will move you well beyond looking good to looking fantastic.

Play Up Your Strengths

If you have great legs, make knee-length (or shorter) skirts and dresses your wardrobe staples. A long neck deserves low-cut blouses and lots of V-neck sweaters. Vivid green eyes sparkle even more when you wear the right shades, and toned arms will always get attention in sleeveless tops. Whether you have a beautiful face, sexy cleavage, perfect shoulders or fabulous hair, use clothes to highlight your best features. It's all about adding to (and never taking away from) what you've got.

CAMERON DIAZ showcases her exceptional legs with a micro-minidress and sexy heels.

Develop a Signature Look

Women with memorable style select pieces that become distinctive to their look. You can create a signature that is bold or subtle, such as always wearing something lavender or a favorite stack of bangles. Create a uniform based on what makes you feel your best. Whether it's a basic white shirt and black pants or feminine day dresses, wear some variation of it every day of the year. Repetition isn't boring—it is the mark of a confident woman who knows what she likes and what suits her best.

EVA MENDES isn't shy about exuding sex appeal, as proven by her penchant for decidedly feminine colors and cuts.

Never Under-estimate...

Good Posture

Lifting your head, letting your shoulders drop down and holding your stomach in slightly are simple adjustments that make you look taller, thinner, confident and more elegant. Enough said. Stand up straight!

A Great Haircut

This is crucial; your hair is your constant accessory. The right style brightens your eyes, makes your face prettier and can definitely make you seem younger. Yes, good haircuts can be expensive, but what they add to your overall appearance makes them worth every penny. Get a cut you can manage at all times—not one that looks good only when a professional styles it.

Confidence

Some of the most attractive people in the world are not always the most fashionably dressed, yet they radiate a self-assurance that gets them noticed. While you can quickly lose your poise if you are not comfortable in what you are wearing, the right clothes can lend you some of your attitude. The rest has to come from within.

JESSICA ALBA is a stand-up type of gal, even on casual occasions.

A classic bob has KATIE HOLMES projecting polish.

ALI LARTER has a quality that conveys she's comfortable in her own skin.

21

style for the ages

The last several decades of women's fashion have loosened up the rules for what you should wear at certain stages of life. In the 1960s, for instance, women in their 40s didn't really wear jeans. Today, you'd be hard-pressed to find a 40-year-old who doesn't have a few different pairs in her closet for a variety of occasions. Hooray for progress!

Even with all this fashion freedom, there are still a few guidelines worth following: If you are in your 20s and 30s, build a simple core wardrobe, but also experiment and play with inexpensive, trend-driven items. In your 40s and beyond, establish a lasting wardrobe of the best basics, investing in the highest quality you can afford. Play with your accessories, but also start to collect some real jewelry as well.

Remember, getting older can work to your advantage. With age comes the authority to wear polished clothes that younger women often can't pull off. If you want to wear pencil skirts and high-heeled pumps every day, do it. Years also bring increased confidence and conviction—let your clothes show off those qualities, and leave the baby-doll dresses to the teens.

Ageless Accessories

Certain pieces have no age restrictions and look as sharp on a 20-something as they do on a woman in her 60s.

A Good Bag Classic handbags are worth their hefty price tags because you can carry them for years. You want your basic shades, but also try one in a bright color; if well crafted, a bag is ageless, timeless and fun.

Sunglasses Don't worry about being practical or classic here, because a quick way to update any look is to slip on the latest sunglasses. Plus, who doesn't occasionally like to hide behind a fabulous set of shades?

Jewelry Investment pieces aside, where is the rule that says you have to be young to get away with wearing chunky, statement costume jewelry? These pieces stand out on women of every age.

20s

BLAKE LIVELY can show skin with confidence. At an older age, you might have to pick either the short hem or the exposed shoulder, but for now, just dare to bare and have fun!

40s

30s

50s+

With this youthful take on a classic, GABRIELLE UNION layers a short, belted trenchcoat with bell sleeves over a long, fitted shirt and sexy jeans. The peacock-print bag adds an extra pop.

KRISTIN DAVIS embodies demure sophistication with a white button-front top and black full skirt, but her sexy, red-bow-accented heels provide some welcome playfulness.

With age comes knowledge of how to play up your best physical assets. Here, MICHELLE PFEIFFER accentuates her stunning figure (especially her fantastic shoulders!) with a structured-bodice dress in a neutral hue.

chapter 2

DRESSES

What's not to love about the right dress? It's your do-not-pass-go fast track to fabulous—just slip on and zip. It requires little thought (no separates to coordinate!) yet looks totally pulled together and polished. That said, if you do feel like mixing it up, a dress is a surprisingly versatile canvas for showing off your personal style (add a blazer, add a cardigan, add a leather jacket—lady's choice). Its innate femininity can be an instant mood lifter for you and a crowd pleaser for everyone you encounter. And best of all? It's comfortable.

A menswear blazer contrasts nicely with KEIRA KNIGHTLEY's feminine dress, giving it a more casual look. Slip off the jacket and—presto!—she's ready for a night out.

EVA LONGORIA PARKER's figure-hugging shift (in a shade that complements her skin tone) provides a clean foundation for an eye-popping necklace and oh-so-sexy heels.

Even a highly adorned dress can work for daytime if paired, as CAMILLA BELLE does here, with a leather belt and unembellished shoes. (This look works best with a short dress.)

ZOE SALDANA transforms her simple, streamlined dress into an evening standout by pairing it with vivacious platform heels in the same color.

dress style primer

A dress is a dress is a dress? Not quite. Knowing the core silhouettes will help you navigate the options at the store (and in your closet).

Shift

A streamlined dress with slight-to-no waist definition, its hem hits just above or below the knee. It is often sleeveless.

Strapless

A strapless dress might be full or fitted, short or long, but it will always have a bare, no-strap top that shows off the shoulders and décolleté.

Wrap

Taking a cue from the traditional Japanese kimono, the wrap dress crisscrosses the front of the body and ties at the waist. It is a fitted style that flatters many shapes.

Sheath

This is a clean-cut, often sleeveless dress—similar to a shift but fitting closer to the body—with a nipped-in waist and knee-length hemline.

Empire

This style has a high waistline that sits just below the bust. If there are sleeves, they are often narrow for balance.

A-Line

An A-line is a dress with side seams that gently flare from the armhole down to the hemline, giving the dress a tent (or A) shape.

Bias-Cut
Bias has to do with how the fabric is cut—on the diagonal. This allows the dress to naturally follow the body's curves.

Halter
A halter dress is usually back-less and ties at the nape of the neck. Beyond that, it can be long, short, fitted or loose.

Asymmetrical
Whether it has a one-shoulder neckline or an uneven hem that dips on one side, an asymmetrical dress can be romantic or edgy.

Shirtdress

Inspired by the silhouette of a man's button-front shirt, a shirtdress can be collared or not and is often belted.

Full

The full dress has a fitted torso paired with a pleated, ample skirt. Some skirts have layers underneath to give them a bell shape.

dresses: flatter your figure

Which styles will showcase your shape best? Some surefire dressing-room tips.

Shape	Look for	Avoid	Don't Forget
Curvy	Semifitted styles that softly follow your curves and show off your waist-line, including wraps, sheaths, belted shirt-dresses and full dresses.	Anything either too loose or too fitted (including styles that cinch the waist too tightly) and high necklines.	• Choose medium-weight knits and soft fabrics that drape well. • Opt for lower necklines found in wrap, off-the-shoulder or strapless styles. • For a slimming effect, show some skin: Expose legs or cleavage.
Short	Simple silhouettes, such as fitted-sheath, wrap, shirtdress or Empire styles that will accentuate your petite figure without overwhelming it.	Too much embellishment and full skirts.	• The hem length is critical: Keep it just above or below the knee. • Choose looks with vertical details, such as buttons, seams and piping. • Monochromatic styles have a lengthening effect.
Boyish	Belted styles, like shirt-dresses and wrap dresses, that add curves. Not concerned with curves? A-lines and shifts are equally chic options.	Voluminous styles, T-shirt and tank dresses.	• Create curves with bias cuts, draping and ruching. • A-line skirts produce a feminine silhouette. • Slim shifts that skim the knee highlight a trim figure.
Full Bust	Semifitted shapes that have open necklines and nipped-in waists. Shirtdresses, wraps and sheaths fit the bill.	High, off-the-shoulder and boatneck lines; form-less A-lines and tunics; full, gathered sleeves; and styles with wide belts.	• Draw the eye up with V-necks, scoop-necks and sweetheart necklines. • Keep detailing on the top to a minimum. • Try skirts with a slight flare to balance your bust and create motion. • Choose soft fabrics with movement.
Small Bust	Empire, fitted-sheath and strapless styles that can add definition to the bust. A-line, shift and shirtdress options show off a trim silhouette.	Anything with built-in boning or darts you can't fill out.	• Shirring and ruching over the bust will help create fullness. • Shapes with defined and/or belted waists will create the illusion of a bigger bustline.

Shape	Look for	Avoid	Don't Forget
Tummy	Dresses that do not accent the waistline, such as shifts, subtle A-lines, and Empire styles, and dresses with matching jackets or coats.	Anything that accentuates the waist and dresses that are too tight, stiff or bulky.	• Draw attention away from your middle with open necklines. • Monochromatic looks are the most slimming. • Blouson shapes can be flattering.
Short Waist/ Long Legs	Drop-waist styles or anything that obscures the natural waistline, such as a straight sheath.	Stiff fabrics and dresses with belts or other details at the waistline.	• Use deep V-necks to elongate your neckline. • Hemlines are best just above or hovering at the knee. • Drop-waist details, such as seams, create a longer torso.
Long Waist/ Short Legs	Empire styles, semifitted sheaths and A-line dresses.	Anything that accentuates your natural waistline.	• Direct the eye upward and away from the waist with detailing on the top. • Keep hemlines right around or above the knee.

Your Tailor to the Rescue!

• If you need a hem lowered, a tailor can do it if there is enough fabric, if the original hemline isn't discolored, and if that first hemline can be pressed out of the cloth.

• If the armholes are too low, they can be tightened a little underneath on the side seams. If they need more than a little tightening, a tailor has to lift the dress at the shoulder seams, meaning the neck opening might need to be reshaped as well.

• Armholes can also be enlarged on dresses without much detail or tailoring at the front. If the dress has an elaborate shape, adjusting the armholes is probably impossible without ruining its design.

• The shape of a round neckline can sometimes be changed to a V-neck or U-neck.

• If the dress has a waist seam that goes all the way around, the waistline can be moved if there is enough fabric in the bodice.

how to wear it

Most dresses are versatile. Want to dress it up? Dress it down? It's all about the add-ons. Think of this as "dressing your dress," and be ready for your options to multiply.

Layer

What you put over or under your dress can totally transform it. A relatively simple sheath becomes something much more special just by adding a short-sleeved shirt with bow detailing beneath. In colder weather, a turtleneck could also add a fun twist.

Accessorize

Flats, boots, sandals, heels—your choice of footwear can take a simple dress and make it look casual, gamine, tough or elegant. A dress with a clean neckline will show off a statement necklace, and a loose shape can be cinched with an eye-catching belt.

Can a Voluminous Dress Be Sexy?

Definitely, if you keep proportion in mind. The key to avoiding looking dowdy in a tent-style cut is to show off your legs, so shorter is better (at least 3 inches above the knee). This length will also help to counterbalance the expansive width of the garment. The right shoes are important as well. Dainty heels or peep-toes are your best bet for projecting a sexy vibe.

Try Florals

Worried about looking matronly in flower prints? Just go for fabrics that are more modern. If still in doubt, lean on your accessories to keep the outfit fresh. A dark ankle boot or flat sandal dresses a floral down for day; heels that play up a print's color dress it up.

little-black-dress essentials

Women rely on the allure of the LBD for everything from work to dinner dates to holiday galas. While simple options are usually best for day wear, donning your favorite black number after 5 o'clock calls for something with a little more sizzle.

Romantic

Chiffon, lace, tulle, feathers, soft silhouettes and accents including bows and ruffles are the components of highly feminine LBDs.

Nothing says girlie like RACHEL BILSON's ruffled dress and embellished shoes.

Sophisticated

These pieces have architectural seam details and strong lines. They are best for the true minimalist but can be punched up with playful accessories.

LUCY LIU goes for simple chic in this fitted dress paired with standout shoes.

Sexy

Straps, plunging necklines and body-hugging cuts can all help to accentuate your assets. Keep it tasteful—remember, a little goes a long way!

CHARLIZE THERON sizzles in a sea of straps, while classic heels balance the look.

Edgy

Asymmetrical necklines, short hemlines, strap details, grommets, jet beading and hints of leather can lend an LBD a cool edginess.

HEIDI KLUM makes leather look elegant (and shows off her toned upper body too).

JACKETS

chapter 3

A killer jacket is the ultimate wardrobe enhancer: It adds a touch of instant sophistication paired with any other pieces—from jeans to dresses—and, without looking like it's trying too hard, can do wonders for your figure.

Ideally, every closet would boast at least one investment-piece jacket. That's the one made from superior fabric that you took to your tailor so that it's perfectly fitted to your body. But more affordable jackets also play an important role in your look, allowing you to experiment with the latest trends.

A hot-pink cropped jacket in an architectural cut keeps JOY BRYANT looking thoroughly modern, especially when paired with an artsy necklace and platform sandals.

RIHANNA balances out the femininity of her flouncy skirt with a masculine, hip-length motorcycle-style jacket. The super-edgy shoes further play up the jacket's bold stance.

A boyfriend-cut blazer relaxes KEIRA KNIGHTLEY's prim and polished skirt and bow-collared top combination. The jacket's dark hue also doesn't compete with the green skirt.

A jacket in a shimmery, metallic-hued fabric with lapels flipped up provides coverage without compromising elegance in LEIGHTON MEESTER's evening look.

jacket style primer

There is a plethora of jacket cuts available, which means you'll always be able to find at least one that works with any given outfit.

Menswear-Tailored

This single- or double-breasted style can have a classic peaked lapel, and back or side vents.

Tuxedo

A single- or double-breasted black, white or navy jacket echoes the feeling of a men's tuxedo in cut (especially at the lapel) and fabric.

Peplum

A waist-cinching jacket like this features a flared hem and structured shoulders.

Boyfriend

This single- or double-breasted menswear style is oversize and often has rolled-up sleeves.

Military

Although the shape can vary from short to long or from fitted to slightly loose, a military-style jacket usually involves epaulets and brass-button details.

Bomber

A zip-front style often in leather with a slight blouson shape, it tapers at the wrists and at or right below the waist.

Safari

Interpretations can have breast pockets, shoulder snaps and often a belted waist and usually are made in neutrals, such as khaki, army green or black.

jackets: flatter your figure

It's crucial that a jacket fits just so. The first step is finding the right cut for your shape.

Shape	Look for	Avoid	Don't Forget
Curvy	A semifitted style that hits at the point where the hips start to curve out or that just covers the derrière. Belted styles flatter shapely waists.	Cropped shapes and styles that button up to the neck.	• Always choose single-breasted styles. • Look for a closure right below the bustline. • Keep lines simple. • Opt for narrow, not exaggerated, lapels.
Short	Shorter, clean, cropped and/or fitted styles.	Long jackets, double-breasted styles and excessive details.	• Cropped jackets emphasize your waist. • Always choose single-breasted styles. • Opt for one- or two-button closures. • Look for jackets with narrow lapels that end above your natural waist.
Boyish	A fitted, mid-hip length nipped in at the waist. Belted styles are good options.	Anything square or overly boxy.	• Try a peplum style, which creates an hourglass silhouette. • Seams create a narrow-looking waist.
Narrow Shoulders	Cuts with defined, tailored (not soft) shoulders.	Dropped sleeves and seams that start before the edge of your shoulder.	• Peaked shoulders or other details such as epaulets give your shoulders more structure. • Choose sleeves with seams at the edge or slightly beyond your shoulder line. • Small shoulder pads can be a plus.
Broad Shoulders	Longer styles and soft, unstructured jackets that help de-emphasize the shoulders.	Anything that is fitted around or emphasizes the shoulders, such as large lapels, double-breasted styles, breast pockets, epaulets or shoulder details.	• Try deep armholes and raglan, kimono or dropped sleeves to soften shoulders. • Choose V-necks, small lapels, shawl collars and single-breasted styles. • If your hips are narrow, try patch pockets to balance your shoulders.

Shape	Look for	Avoid	Don't Forget
Full Bust	Fitted or semifitted styles that are more open around the neck.	High necklines, double-breasted or belted styles, patch pockets and short, rolled lapels.	• Always go for single-breasted jackets. • Choose contour seams. • Opt for narrow lapels. • Look for a closure right below the bustline—anything lower, and the jacket could gape open.
Small Bust	Fitted jackets nipped in at the waist. Try double-breasted or belted styles. Shrunken jackets that fit right below the waist are great for slim silhouettes.	Jackets with a covered placket.	• Use draping, breast pockets, seams and shirring to enhance a smaller bustline. • High necklines offer chic options. • Select jackets with feminine details such as puffy or bracelet sleeves.
Tummy	Semifitted or straight-cut styles that reach below the derrière—or even longer.	Cropped jackets, patch pockets, double-breasted styles and exaggerated collars and lapels.	• Try to keep all details vertical and narrow. • Use a deep V-cut jacket to elongate the torso. • Opt for single-breasted closures.

Your Tailor to the Rescue!

- The most common fix is to shorten or lengthen the sleeves; usually they should end an inch past your wristbone.

- Lapels can be cut down and even reshaped.

- A jacket can be changed from a three-button closure to a two-button version.

- Shoulders can be reshaped by taking out padding, leaving a more natural silhouette.

- A jacket can be shortened, and seams taken out where there is enough fabric.

how to wear it

A jacket can go in many different directions. Get extra mileage from it by trying these proven styling tricks.

Contrast Masculine and Feminine

Mix your men's-style cuts with feminine elements. Pair a wool pinstripe blazer with a sheer ruffled blouse or cocktail dress. Alternately, a feminine jacket complements a tailored top and pants or a simple sheath.

Get the Balance Right

For the best length and proportion, look to the short-over-long and long-over-short guidelines (see Chapter 1). Pair a cropped shape (short) with a single-color sheath or with pants and a top of the same color (long). A longer jacket works best over a shorter skirt or narrow pants.

Instant Jacket Update

Try a belt with a lightweight blazer.
Whether it is a slim model or a wider version, a belt is a great way to highlight your waist and freshen up your wardrobe.

Add a scarf or bold brooch.
The right scarf can add dimension to your look and provide a shot of color that will complement a neutral base. An arty brooch also draws the eye up. It can be either modern or vintage, but bigger is better for real impact. Choose scarves in lightweight weaves and pastels for summer and in heavier cashmeres and wools for winter.

Keep Colors in Mind

Dark neutral jackets work with anything from jeans to dresses. A jacket in a lighter, brighter shade can soften up a classic neutral top worn underneath. Keep the look modern and steer clear of big jackets in shout-out shades; if you do go bold, keep the shape fitted and/or cropped.

the classic:
FITTED BLAZER

Though it comes from the world of menswear, a tailored blazer is anything but masculine on a woman. You'll pay more for good tailoring, but a blazer that fits you perfectly adds instant polish to any look, and is authoritative, sexy and elegant.

1: Collars and lapels, regardless of size (from superwide to very narrow), should always lie perfectly flat; they should never bunch up at any point. Classic lapels traditionally are about 2 inches wide.

2: The shoulder line of your blazer should rest exactly at, or just slightly beyond, the curve of your shoulder. A classic fit has the seam falling $\frac{1}{2}$ to $\frac{1}{4}$ inch outside the shoulder.

3: When a blazer fits properly, there should never be any pulling or tugging of the fabric near the buttons, and buttoning should be easy. Also, the jacket should taper just slightly at your waistline.

4: Traditional sleeves should also taper slightly but should never feel snug. They should be long enough to cover your wristbones when your hands are hanging down at your sides.

1......

2............

.........3

4
....

SUITS

chapter 4

Stuffy? Far from it. Suits are powerful style boosters that, in the right shapes and proper proportions, can do wonders for any figure and telegraph a wide range of moods, from flirty (a fitted cap-sleeve skirt-suit combo) to sophisticated cool (a skinny black pantsuit paired with low-top sneakers) to every attitude in between. A few choice suits can be the perfect base on which a stylish woman builds her entire wardrobe, always providing her with just the right ensemble for work, a job interview, a dinner date, cocktails or even a black-tie affair. And talk about flexible! Your suit components love nothing more than to be mixed and matched with the other items in your closet. Playing well with others? Now that's anything but uptight.

The high-waist cut and floor-length cuffs of this suit's pants make JESSICA BIEL's legs look longer, while the defined shoulders and fitted jacket show off her shapely physique.

JENNIFER LOPEZ wraps up in a tailored, double-breasted suit that still allows for a little décolletage. Glitzy hoop earrings add a cool finishing touch to her crisp white look.

SALMA HAYEK covers up her top half but doesn't lose an ounce of feminine appeal in this sexy calf-revealing skirt suit. The cinched waist emphasizes her hourglass shape.

While the stovepipe trousers of MARIA BELLO's three-piece tweed suit highlight her legs, the buttoned vest and belt also draw some attention to her narrow middle.

suit style primer

Suits come in a wide variety of shapes and looks (pantsuits, skirt suits, dress suits), but for the most part, you could group any given style into one of these three categories.

Tailored

Whether the bottom is pants or a skirt, a tailored suit features a structured jacket and an overall slim silhouette. Jackets are often single- or double-breasted and cut close to the body. Pants can be long and fluid or cropped and slightly pegged; pencil or slight A-line skirts are usually the other bottom options.

Feminine

This softer version of the suit can run the gamut. Jackets can be cropped and/or blouson, have draping or seam details, and sport bell-shaped or bracelet-length sleeves. Though sometimes worn with soft, pleated pants, a feminine jacket is most often paired with a skirt that is fitted or full.

Three Must-Dos for Suit Care

1 Place your pieces on proper hangers. Jackets need those with molded ends; pants should be folded at the crease on pants hangers and skirts hung on skirt hangers. Storing clothes improperly can quickly ruin them by straining the fabric. A wire hanger can make an outward and sometimes irreparable dent in the shoulder of your jacket.

2 Don't confuse rumpled with dirty. Dry-cleaning your suit a few times per season is all that it needs. Clean it more often, and you'll wear out the fabric and seams. Instead, air out the suit and then steam it. Invest in a home steamer or take your suit to the dry cleaner for steaming only. Avoid ironing; it can flatten lapels, leave imprint outlines of the inner construction of the suit on the outside, and turn some fabrics shiny.

3 Always launder the top and bottom of a suit together. Because dry-cleaning can be harsh on fabrics, you want the matching pieces to wear at the same rate. If you dry-clean one piece more often, eventually your suit could end up mismatched.

Evening

Whether the jacket is matched with pants or a skirt, the factors that distinguish an evening suit are usually the fabric and details. Silks, satins and other luxury materials can make for elegant evening options, while decorative frills (such as ruffles, peekaboo bits of lace, beading, and embroidery) are other sophisticated nighttime elements.

suits: flatter your figure

Make sure this wardrobe investment perfectly highlights everything you've got.

Shape	Look for	Avoid	Don't Forget
Curvy	Fluid fabrics that float over curves and jackets that highlight the waist.	Boxy or cropped jackets that hide your waistline, and voluminous shapes or too much fabric.	• Make sure both pieces are fitted but not tight. • A single-breasted jacket is most slimming. • Pants should have a straight or slightly flared leg. • Choose a skirt with a flat front.
Narrow Shoulders	Jackets with shawl collars or wider lapels paired with slim and simple pants and skirts.	Suits where the bottom half is fuller and wider than the jacket, and jackets that are snug at the shoulders.	• Peaked, slightly padded shoulders will balance the look. • Opt for shirts that are open or can be unbuttoned at the neck; they will widen the chest and shoulder area. • Belt the jacket to define your waist.
Broad Shoulders	Feminine jackets with soft shoulders and tailored styles, as long as the sleeves are narrow and not full. Raglan sleeves also flatter.	Blouson sleeves and big collars or ruffles around the neckline.	• Too-narrow jacket shoulders will only widen the look of yours. • Try wearing a light-colored blouse with a collar under a jacket to draw the eye to the center of the body.
Short Waist/ Long Legs	Longer jacket lengths that hit below the waist and obscure it, creating balance.	Cropped or belted jackets and high-waist pants.	• Emphasize your leg length with narrow pants and slim or short skirts. • Choose jacket details that draw the eye up. • Monochromatic suits create head-to-toe visual length. • High, narrow lapels are best.
Long Waist/ Short Legs	Suits with fluid pants or skirts and cropped or belted jackets.	Longer jackets with skirts that end at the knee, cropped pants and mid-calf skirts.	• High-waist pants and skirts lengthen the legs. • A long jacket over a short skirt can be a good proportion. • The reverse—a cropped jacket with longer pants—is equally flattering.

Shape	Look for	Avoid	Don't Forget
Large Top/Small Bottom	Softer, more feminine jackets, as opposed to tailored ones.	Padding or excessive details on the jacket.	• V-necks and narrow lapels lengthen the torso. • Slim jackets that hit just around your hips work well. • Fabrics with drape, as opposed to structure, can flatter. • Slim (but not tight) pants are best. • Hem details on skirts can add flair.
Round Middle/Thin Legs	Jackets that are cut close to the body but aren't fitted at the waist.	Jacket styles that emphasize the waist, whether with buttons, seams or a belt.	• Focus the attention on your legs with pencil skirts and narrow pants. • Details at the neckline are well placed to draw attention. • Choose slim, not blouson, sleeves. • Keep whatever is underneath (blouse, tank top, etc.) clean and simple.
Small Top/Large Bottom	Suit details or accessories (such as a brooch) at the top of the jacket and a simple bottom half.	Skirts that hug the hips too tightly or have flouncy, ruffled or complicated hems.	• Show your waistline by wearing a fitted jacket that hits several inches below or above your hips. • Full sleeves can help to balance out your proportions.

Your Tailor to the Rescue!

- Accept that finding an off-the-rack suit that fits you perfectly is highly improbable, then get comfortable with the idea of alterations—you're going to need them to do your suits justice.

- Ask around for recommendations for a tailor in your area who is good with suits.

- See advice on dresses (p. 31), jackets (p. 41), pants (p. 77), and skirts (p. 99) for specifics on what can and cannot be altered.

how to wear it

A suit can have nine lives—at least!—depending on exactly what you add into the mix. Some helpful guidelines for selecting just the right elements.

Savvy and Chic

Look for styles that truly reflect your personality. A sleeveless jacket not only shows off sexy arms—it telegraphs a playful energy. Relaxed, tie-front cuffed trousers reinforce the notion that you're anything but the business-as-usual type.

Make It Work

Just because you're climbing the ladder of professional success doesn't mean you should dress in a ho-hum manner. Try an eye-catching, retro-cut jacket paired with a basic-cut skirt and one or two accessories, such as sleek high heels and a chunky bracelet.

Get More Bang for Your Buck

Optimizing your dollar when it comes to suit buying boils down to two things: material and number of components. For material, look for a seasons-spanning fabric such as a lightweight wool. As for components, if your budget allows, get the matching skirt/dress and pants. Not only can you wear your suit year-round, but you also might find yourself wearing combinations more than once a week. Ka-ching!

Dress It Up

A white suit can prove the perfect canvas for your favorite night-on-the-town accessories. A feminine, dark shirt pops here, providing a stark and provocative contrast. Bold necklaces add texture and oomph, while a small handbag and strappy sandals in a quiet shade add polish.

what to wear under a suit

While guys are pretty much still limited to wearing tailored shirts, T-shirts and turtlenecks under their suits, women have almost limitless options. That said, be sure that your top flatters both you and your suit.

Perhaps the best way to maximize your suit's potential is to have at least two or three different tops available. A V-neck cashmere sweater, a button-front cotton shirt or a chiffon blouse in a feminine print are all nice options.

Buying a collared, button-front shirt requires the most thought. The collar should complement your jacket. If it has a rounded collar, it will compete with your jacket's pointed one. It's always best to stick to matching shapes. Buy a top when you're buying a suit, or take the jacket along when you're looking for something to pair with it. This is the best way to make sure the pieces match as well as you picture in your mind's eye.

When wearing sleeves under your suit, be sure they fit under your jacket without bunching. Ultimately, the bottom of the sleeves should peep out of (or be very close to) the cuffs of your jacket. Another alternative is a sleeveless top. In either case, make sure the shirt is long enough so it stays put when you move around or sit down.

Taking a Suit from Day to Night

Dressing up your suit is a cinch. If you're wearing a tailored number, switch the top under your jacket for something a bit more seductive, whether it is a lace camisole or chiffon blouse—or if your jacket isn't too revealing when buttoned, opt for wearing nothing at all underneath. Next, swap out your day shoes for something either delicate or daring (such as peep-toe stilettos or strappy platform sandals), your totebag for a clutch, and your daytime jewelry for one standout piece.

A black necktie blouse contrasts in color and femininity with **MARISA TOMEI**'s crisp white tailored suit. The fitted waist conveys sexiness even though she's totally covered up.

Shorts Suits

For ultimate summer comfort without sacrificing style, suits that feature shorts are a sexy option. Shorts can be paired with long or short jackets. (If you do wear shorts to an office, make sure they hit no higher than just above the knee.)

With gold hoops, a few necklaces and an open ruffled neckline, SHERYL CROW avoids looking masculine in a tuxedo-inspired evening suit. A small handbag with gold details plays off of her accessories.

ANNE HATHAWAY's long jacket over a loose shirt and shorts is casual but not messy. Simple necklaces and bright lipstick also add polish. And check out those heels! (For shoe advice, see Chapter 13.)

CHARLIZE THERON sports a structured cropped jacket with classic-cut shorts. Left untucked, the long, fitted shirt provides visual balance while also lengthening her torso.

the classic:
TAILORED SUIT

A well-crafted suit is potentially one of the biggest wardrobe investments you can make, so when shopping, you want to find one that is flattering and shows the telltale signs of quality. Be patient and hold out for the best—you'll thank yourself later.

1: Most lapels sit flat and begin to roll just above the uppermost button. If the lapel gapes, the suit is too small in the back and chest and can only be fixed if there is enough material to let out the seams.

2: Opt for a material that is multiseasonal (such as lightweight wool). While the most well-made suits have all-silk linings, what's important is that the lining lies flush with the suit.

3: Pants should hang straight from the waist to the foot. A 17- to 19-inch opening at the bottom of the leg is classic. If you see the outline of a pocket through the pants, it means they are too tight.

4: When judging pants length, be sure to walk around in the shoes you will wear most. The hem of classic-cut pants should touch the instep in front and slope down to cover half your heel.

1.......................

2.............

3........

4........

COATS

chapter 5

A good coat is practical—it keeps elements out and warmth in—but a great coat also ups your style quotient. And unless you live in a tropical climate, most likely you'll want to build a separate wardrobe of coats to meet your needs. Consider these basic five types when shopping: workday, weekend, raincoat, evening coat and one for the extreme cold. Although a keeper will cost you, if you truly love it and reach for it often, it becomes a bargain.

A three-quarter-sleeve coat means CHRISTINA RICCI can showcase what's layered beneath, adding a bit of color and texture. Cinching the waist with a belt gives some shape.

HILARY SWANK steps out at night in a vibrant, dressy variation on a traditional trenchcoat. She shows off her personal style by buckling the self-belt off to one side.

A tailored black coat gets a modern update with THANDIE NEWTON's bright-red strappy heels. The flare of the coat also lends a feminine swing to the otherwise classic cut.

A short, unstructured day coat over a shorter dress reveals IVANKA TRUMP's long legs and is sexy without seeming vulgar. The colorful clutch makes it modern.

coat style primer

Coats are not just necessities—they're also immediate attention-grabbers. So consider your outer layer a reflection of your inner style.

Peacoat

Derived from a style worn by sailors, the peacoat typically hits below the hip and is double-breasted.

Car

This above-the-knee coat has a classic appeal. It typically features buttons running down the front but can also have a double-breasted closure.

Military

A reinterpretation of traditional military coats, it is usually long (from below the knee to the ankle) and double-breasted, most often with brass-button details.

Cape →
A sleeveless style that can have arm-holes, it can be belted or have a hood.

Wrap ↙
This style of coat has extra material that allows it to overlap in the front. It is cinched by a belt.

Topcoat →
This traditional button-front cut hangs from the shoulders and features a fold-over collar and side pockets.

Parka
A puffy, often down-filled jacket, this casual style ranges from cropped to below midcalf.

Trenchcoat
This classic double-breasted raincoat has become a fashion staple (see p. 70).

Cocoon
This roomy coat is often cut above the knee and has sleeves that aren't full-length.

Toggle

Usually cut from wool, this coat has front toggle closures and often a hood.

Bracelet-Sleeve

Long or short, this coat has sleeves that end somewhere between elbow and mid-forearm.

Chesterfield

Slim, with blazerlike lapels (sometimes in velvet), this is a men's-style single- or double-breasted coat.

coats: flatter your figure

The perfect coat covers you up while still accentuating your best attributes.

Shape	Look for	Avoid	Don't Forget
Curvy	Straight or belted styles, like wraps, with simple lines that hit near the knee.	Flap or patch pockets, high necklines and styles that are too full or too fitted.	• Opt for natural-looking shoulder padding. • Use narrow lapels tapered to the waist to create the illusion of height. • Simple, single-breasted coats give a streamlined look.
Short	A style that hovers just at the knee.	Long coats, voluminous or double-breasted styles, wide lapels and excess flourish or detail.	• Elongate your frame with Empire waists, belts or styles with fitted bodices. • Keep lines simple. • Detailed but not overdone necklines draw the eye up.
Boyish	Princess-shaped silhouettes or coats with a defined waistline.	Styles that are too full and have exaggerated shoulder details.	• If you're slim but short, keep hemlines slightly above the knee. • Coats with seamed bodices can give you shape.
Narrow Shoulders	Coats with defined shoulders: slight padding and perhaps some details.	Dropped or raglan sleeves and unstructured styles that allow the fabric to fall at your natural shoulder line.	• Wide necklines and lapels are flattering. • Keep the bottom half of the coat slim. • Belt to emphasize your waist and focus attention away from your top. • Double-breasted versions work.
Broad Shoulders	Loose, unstructured jackets. Go with a length that is mid-hip or longer.	Double-breasted styles, high or closed necks, and top details such as breast pockets, trimming, epaulets and shoulder pads.	• Use deep armholes and raglan sleeves to soften shoulders. • Opt for V-necks with small lapels or narrow collars. • Choose a detailed hem for balance. • Steer clear of stiff fabrics.

Shape	Look for	Avoid	Don't Forget
Full Bust	Semifitted, single-breasted styles with deep V-necks, and narrow lapels that taper to the waist.	High necklines, patch pockets and double-breasted styles that draw the eye up.	• Fitted waists are fine as long as the seams aren't too high and the cut isn't too tight. • Full sleeves will only add pounds. • Use high armholes and a natural shoulder to create a slimmer silhouette.
Small Bust	Styles with a nipped waist or a belt; tailored cuts are also good options.	Anything too square or boxy that will leave you with a nondescript silhouette.	• Go with flattering details on top, such as pockets, wide lapels, and seams or draping at the shoulders and down the front. • High armholes keep the style from being overpowering.
Tummy	Straight-cut, single-breasted, tailored styles, or a subtle A-line shape.	Double-breasted styles, anything fitted at the mid-section, and pocket details near the waist.	• Try high armholes and a natural shoulder to create a slimmer silhouette. • Go with a mid-hip length or longer. • Choose coats with simple closures—no oversize buttons or toggles that can pull.

Your Tailor to the Rescue!

- When you try your coat on for a tailor, do so wearing the heaviest sweater or blazer you plan to have on underneath. Otherwise the coat can end up being too tight.
- Basic alterations include shortening and lengthening sleeves. Hems can often be raised.
- Seams on the back of the coat can be let out (fabric allowing) and taken in, but doing so by more than 2 inches will require resetting the sleeves—a costly endeavor.

how to wear it

Letting your coat just be an afterthought is missing the perfect opportunity to be fabulous. Instead, think of it as an integrated element of your ensemble.

Sharp Lines

You can never go wrong having at least one highly tailored coat in your closet. With heels and skinny pants, it can go to the office and beyond. Go for hardware-heavy accents for a look that really comes to atten-*tion!*

Bright and Bold

A colorful coat is an immediate pick-me-up. If you've never worn so much color at once, start by pairing it with neutrals underneath. Then, when you're ready to up the ante, try your hand at bold color mixes. In this case, your accessories should stay subdued.

The Hem Rule

That age-old edict that your coat must be about ½ inch longer than your skirt? Well, modern rules are a lot more fluid, so that's not an absolute anymore. While it depends on the style of the coat and skirt, generally you're safe if the skirt is longer than the coat by at least an inch, or vice versa. Calf-grazing coats are great with long, lean pants, and a voluminous shape is best offset with something narrow. For the rest, you have to rely on your mirror and sense of proportion to figure out what looks most flattering.

The Glamorous Coat

Choose an evening coat as you would a gown: You want one rich in detail and cut from luxe material so you feel gorgeous every time you slip it on. You can even make it a standout piece by opting for a print or embroidery. If you need your coat to match several outfits, choose a single, rich shade, then let your accessories add the extra sparkle.

evening drama

Give your parka the night off! Choosing a coat to wear over a cocktail dress or gown is a great opportunity to flaunt a spectacular piece.

Timeless Beauty

For those occasions when you want to feel elegant above all else, a classic style with a vintage appeal is your go-to coat. Look for subtle embellishments or cuts that have a retro sensibility, such as an exaggerated shawl collar or ruffled edges, which can add just the right amount of detail. A quiet color that doesn't compete with whatever you are wearing underneath is usually best.

Something Wild

An animal-print coat is so chic, so mysterious, so fantastically outrageous, it almost doesn't matter what you put on underneath, but we suggest you keep it simple, like a black or other neutral-hued dress. If a whole coat is too much pattern for your taste, try an animal-print wrap or shawl in a thinner fabric. Keep everything else simple and monochromatic for the most impact.

KATHERINE HEIGL, in this wide-collared coat, exudes a ladylike air.

DEBRA MESSING lets her coat do the roaring, while everything else is toned down.

Color It In

A coat in a single saturated shade is both festive and fabulous. It also makes a statement when the combination of the style, color, fabric or details is unexpected, like a trench in gold metallic leather with a studded belt (wow!). The one caveat here: Choose a shade that flatters you *and* what you're wearing underneath. It's a lot of fabric (and a big investment) to have in the wrong hue.

EMMY ROSSUM's red trench flatters her fair skin and dark hair. Quiet heels don't distract.

Casual Evening

When you want to be dressed up but not overdressed, try a day coat with a little more pizzazz. A cape is a clean and elegant option that works as well over a cocktail dress as it does with jeans and a blouse. A dark, wrap-style coat is sleek, while a cocoon or three-quarter-sleeve style in a metallic fabric is equally night-time savvy.

VICTORIA BECKHAM tops a sheath with a cape in a contrasting color for ultimate impact.

the classic:
BELTED TRENCH

The trenchcoat was created for British soldiers at the start of WWI. After the war, in a testament to the practicality and inherent style of this coat, soldiers brought them home and had them shortened to wear to work. The rest, as they say, is fashion history.

1: The wide collar is not only there because it looks good—it can also be turned up, and the large hook and eye at the center closed, to keep the elements out and insulate the wearer.

2: Allow room for easy and comfortable movement when purchasing a trench. You should be able to raise your hands over your head without the trench pulling too tightly across your back.

3: Want to look more refined? Just buckle the belt of your trenchcoat. To add some flair, tie the belt into a single- or double-loop bow; for effortless elegance, tie in a crisp knot.

4: Trenchcoats come in many lengths. Generally, when you'll be wearing it with dresses, choose a longer version; when matched with pants and jeans, a shorter shape is a better pick.

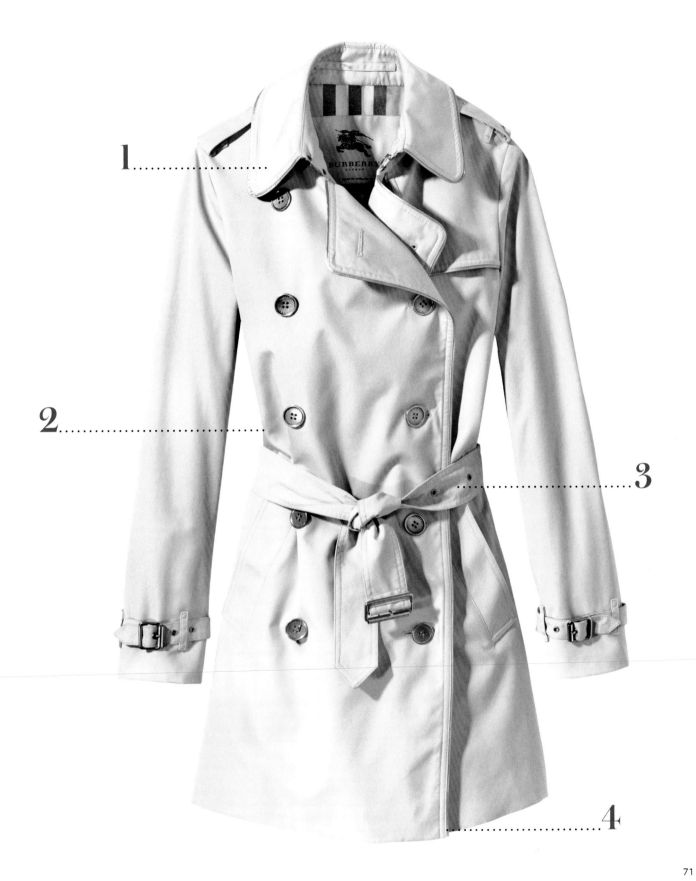

1 ....

2 ....

3 ....

4 ....

PANTS

chapter 6

Hard to believe there was a time in the not-too-distant past when women wearing trousers was simply unacceptable—talk about a crime of fashion! Fortunately, pants are now welcome just about everywhere, which is good news considering they're comfortable, provide great coverage and, in certain cuts, can make your legs look miles long. And depending on the style and fabric, they can even fit the black-tie bill.

Because pants are a go-to basic, having a wide variety of styles in your closet will yield endless outfit possibilities. A good guideline worth remembering is to own at least two pairs of black pants in different fits (such as a classic boot-cut version and a wide-leg model). Just these two options will pair nicely with a variety of jacket cuts and tops. Follow up by filling out your pants wardrobe with other styles, such as cropped, pleated and sporty. Then you'll really have a leg up.

High-waist, narrow pants reveal CHLOE SEVIGNY's svelte shape. The high-collar ruffled blouse, compact clutch and red lips work together to telegraph pure elegance.

MILLA JOVOVICH elevates wide-leg trousers to something truly special with an eye-catching red sash. A fitted, short-sleeve jacket also draws attention to her narrow waist.

Stepping out with her trademark sex appeal, HALLE BERRY's extra-long, skinny leather pants and dark heels lengthen legs, especially paired with a cropped, fitted vest.

ELLEN POMPEO plays up her lean silhouette in classic pants topped with a plunging blouse. The high-waist-low-neckline combo draws eyes to her slim middle.

pants style primer

When it comes to trousers, there's no shortage of options. Is your preference for boot-cut over cropped? High-waist over pleated? Is thin always "in" for you?

Skinny

Super-sleek with a leg that tapers, these are for women who are comfortable showing off the shape of their legs.

Cropped

Usually narrow or pleated, cropped trousers can make your legs look lean, but they don't add much length unless you wear a pair of heels. They also look great with ballet flats.

Pleated

Pleats can vary from tailored menswear-inspired styles to softer, slouchier versions.

High-Waist

High-waist pants are for those who really want to show off their waistline. They often have an inches-wide waistband, and their bottom half can be fluid or fitted.

Wide-Leg

Either soft, slouchy and pleated or flat-front and fitted at the top, wide-leg pants can hide a multitude of sins. They are best worn with chunky heels or high-heeled booties.

Boot-Cut

A flattering go-to style that many women rely on to create a long silhouette, boot-cut pants have a slight flare below the knee.

pants: flatter your figure

Want to find a pair of pants that does you a favor? Then focus on the fit.

Shape	Look for	Avoid	Don't Forget
Curvy	Classic flat-front, boot-cut trousers that sit at or right below your natural waist, or flattering side- or back-zip pants.	Super-tapered styles, front pleats, which will only add pounds, and cuffed hems.	• Wear pants with a slight flare and heels for length. • Thin belts are best worn at the waistband rather than low-slung.
Short	Lean shapes that hit below the ankle and those with minimal or no pleating in front.	Wide-leg and other voluminous styles, as well as super-skinny or cropped pants (unless they are worn with heels).	• Always wear pants slightly long and with heels. • Match tops to bottoms. • Skinny belts that match pants give definition. • Dark colors are preferable.
Boyish	Flat-front trousers that are straight from waist to hem, or high-waist styles.	Pants that are tight on top, which can give your hips an unattractive, square look if your hips and waist are similar in size.	• A slight flare at the hem works for you. • If you want to create curves, try pleats or tapered pants. • Consider low-slung pants as an option. • A wider belt at the waist also creates curves.
Tummy	Longer styles that have soft pleating in the front.	Wearing belts in contrasting shades, high-waist styles and distinctive pocket details.	• Choose pants with either no waistband or one that is an inch or less wide. • If you have slim legs and a small behind, consider narrow side-zip or back-zip pants worn with a longer top. • Flared legs are OK, but avoid cuffs.
Short Waist/ Long Legs	Flat-front styles with slightly lower waists.	Cropped pants, high-waist styles and waistbands that hit at the middle part of your stomach.	• Pants that flare at the bottom will draw the eye away from your waist. • Wear jackets and longer tops that can be left untucked. • Don't wear a top that contrasts sharply in color with your pants.

Shape	Look for	Avoid	Don't Forget
Long Waist/ Short Legs	Classic trousers that sit at or slightly above your natural waistline and have straight or flared legs.	Low-waist styles and cropped pants.	• Tuck in your top only if your pants have a slightly high waist. • Pleated trousers worn with soft blouses can camouflage your middle. • Longer hems with heels will lengthen the legs.
Flat Bottom	Boot-cut, skinny or high-waist styles that are fitted around the backside.	Overly baggy shapes, especially those with lots of pleating.	• Use pockets, back yokes and stitching to accent hips and derrière. • Try pants with stretch to help play up curves. • Wear heels to give your bottom a lift. • Tuck in shirts to help define your waist.
Large Bottom	Well-tailored, flat-front or single-pleat trousers with wider legs that allow enough movement through the hips and thighs.	Back pockets that are too small or far apart. Also avoid: super-wide-leg pants, anything too tapered, and high-waist or low-slung styles.	• A slight flare can help balance your silhouette. • The waistband should be no more than an inch wide and should sit at or just below your waist. • Consider sewing up side pockets.

Your Tailor to the Rescue!

- Sometimes you can buy a pair of pants straight off the rack without getting them altered—but it's important to get the length right.
- Pants can also be made longer, but how much longer is determined by the size of the hem. Take the shoes (flat or heeled) you plan on wearing with you to the tailor to ensure proper length.
- Pants legs and waists can be tapered.
- Hips and legs can sometimes be widened.
- A tailor can add lining to heavy materials, but it is not recommended for anything too light, as it will probably show through.

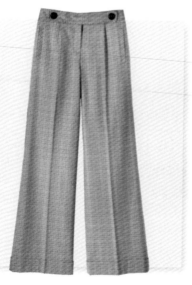

how to wear it

From a day at the office to a night on the town, pants are your go-anywhere—and go-with-everything—option.

Classic Cut

The best pants to take you to the boardroom and beyond are classic and have few details. A cuffed trouser style will look sharp with pumps. No need to wear a matching jacket—instead, try one with more flourish and/or a top with some interesting elements to add texture to the look.

Casual Chic

For brunch or museum-hopping, pull out pants in a casual material (such as cotton poplin). In lieu of a jacket, try a cardigan or V-neck sweater in an unexpected color. Your shoe choice can be fun as well, whether it is flats or peep-toe pumps.

Pants Perfect: Three Trouser Musts

1 Pants should not bag underneath or be pulled too tight across your behind. If you must compromise, however, do so on the side of a looser fit. That way, the pants will fall straight and give you a trimmer appearance.

2 When it comes to rise, if the crotch hangs too low, it will cut down the leg length and make you look dowdy. If too high, it can be uncomfortable and unsightly.

3 There should be no pulling at the closure of the waistband, and the band should not fold in on itself when you sit. Generally, the most flattering waistline falls an inch above or below the belly button.

Dressing Up Basics

When it comes to dressing up a pair of pants, simpler shapes are often better. Sleek black pants or a pair with tuxedo stripes are evening-worthy options that can be worn in countless ways. Add shimmer and femininity with metallic, beaded or ruffled tops.

the right proportions

Even if your pants fit well, if they're too short (high-water waders, anyone?), dragging in the dirt, or paired with the wrong shoes, you won't look pulled together. Let these guidelines help.

RACHEL BILSON's tan boots complement the brown hue of her jacket.

Hem Length

For straight, flared or wide-leg pants, your hem should always hover about an inch from the ground when you're wearing shoes. This means that if you plan to wear your pants with heels, they have to be hemmed according to the height of your shoes. It also means you will probably need different pants to wear with flats and heels. Cropped pants can hit above or below the ankle, depending on your preference.

What Shoes Work

While fashion guidelines have loosened up in this area, there are still some helpful parameters. Slim, straight-leg pants look best with stilettos, day pumps, ballet flats, streamlined medium-heeled boots or loafers. Wide-leg trousers need something chunkier with a heel to balance their width. Skinny pants can be flattering with flats, as well as with both delicate and more aggressive-looking heels. In colder weather, they also look great tucked into knee-high boots. Casual cropped pants are best with flats or low to medium heel heights, though some versions look fresh with more substantial heels or booties.

CHARLIZE THERON shows just the right amount of shoe.

Pants Dilemmas Q&A

Can you tuck a shirt into second-skin pants?
It's not the best idea, just because you'll see the outline of the shirt. Instead, top your tightest pants with a tunic or, if you want to show your shape, an untucked, skinny-ribbed sweater that skims the upper body but still gives you breathing room.

What can I pair with full trousers to keep them from looking frumpy?
Full trousers look best with a fitted top, such as a cashmere sweater or a tucked-in slim shirt.

What tops flatter high-waist pants best?
To get the maximum look-good benefit, you need to show the top of your waistband. If you're not used to highlighting your midsection, ease into the idea by experimenting with a dressy tissue-weight T left untucked under a cropped jacket or cardigan.

shorts story

Because, in general, dress codes have relaxed, shorts can be acceptable summer alternatives for some casual workplaces (just make sure they aren't too short), as well as for going out at night. Here's what to look for.

Bermudas

This tapered style can hit from mid-thigh to just above the knee, depending on what looks best on you. It is flattering to most women of all ages, and if worn in a solid color with a jacket or cardigan, can be suitable work attire.

Short Shorts

Really for the young and more daring at heart, this less-is-more option is best for weekend activities or evenings out. Full styles take on the appearance of a miniskirt and, when paired with a tucked-in blouse and jacket, have a polished yet flirty appeal. Flat sandals always work, or try heels if you dare. For a bit of an edge, consider ankle boots.

CARRIE UNDERWOOD balances out short shorts with a high-neck top.

Sporty Pants

Want to be comfy for weekend errands? Skip the sweats, please! No need to skimp on style with so many casual-trouser options.

Cargo or utility pants feature practical details, including pockets, snaps, and drawstring waists and hems, among others. Shapes range from baggy, low-slung styles to more streamlined, curve-hugging versions. For balance, contrast fits, such as loose pants paired with a slim top. If your cargos are fitted, however, try a loose blazer, slouchy T-shirt and strappy sandals.

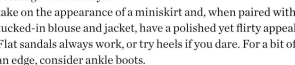

JENNIFER ANISTON pairs a slim tank with loose-fitting pants.

JEANS

chapter 7

Nothing epitomizes American style more than jeans—they're comfortable, uncontrived, casual and oh-so-sexy. No matter how many designer dresses and fabulous accessories you might have, your best-fitting pair of jeans is quite often the item you treasure (and wear) more than anything else you have stashed in your closet.

It's typical for women to have a mini-wardrobe of jeans styles that run the gamut from weekend casual or workwear appropriate to nighttime sexy. Finding variety in this category is easy—there are more denim options than Levi Strauss could ever have dreamt possible—but finding the right fit is very often a true challenge. Yes, trying on a kazillion pairs is annoying, but the payoff is well worth this temporary pain in the rear.

JENNIFER LOPEZ understands the laws of proportion: The flare in her white jeans is balanced by a full, relaxed knit sweater belted at the waist and dark platform shoes.

Dark, super-skinny jeans make ASHLEY OLSEN's legs look super-slim, while the low-slung waist accentuates hips. Chunky sandals toughen up the traditional button-front.

Cropped jeans mean all eyes stay on SARAH JESSICA PARKER's pink pumps. The longer jacket provides a continuous vertical line, making her body look narrow and tall.

CAMERON DIAZ's faded and distressed skinny jeans are a tomboy contrast to her otherwise ladylike look: flirty, polka-dot top, bright red clutch and platform peep-toes.

jeans style primer

Are you the skinny-jeans type, strictly a boot-cut lover, or do you covet your boyfriend's pair? There's a style of jeans out there that will prove absolutely perfect for you.

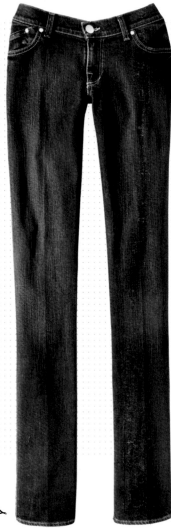

Trouser
With classic flat-front details, this smart version can fit in beautifully at the workplace.

Straight-Leg
Classic and versatile, the standard straight-leg width is 17 inches. In dark rinses, this style can be dressy; in washed and/or distressed denim, it has a relaxed appeal.

Boot-Cut
Similar to the straight-leg but slightly wider from the calf down, this style is one of the most universally flattering—and is easily dressed up with a pair of heels.

Boyfriend

Slouchy, often distressed, and with rolled cuffs, these are great weekend jeans that look best when offset with feminine tops and shoes.

High-Waist

This more fashion-forward alternative is often belted and looks best with heels (for the illusion of even more height) or bold flats.

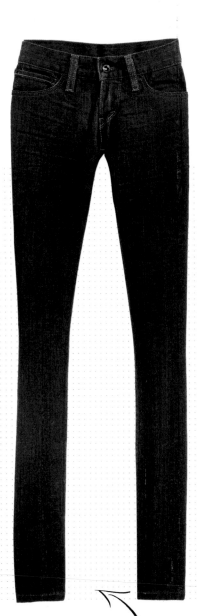

Skinny

Without question the sexiest of all jeans styles, these look great tucked into boots by day and paired with strappy heels by night.

jeans: flatter your figure

For jeans to fit right, they must both hug you and let you go—in all the right places.

Shape	Look for	Avoid	Don't Forget
Curvy	Styles with at least a bit of stretch and straight or flared legs. You might have to fit your hips and behind, then have a tailor take in the waist.	Super-low-cut styles that will sit mid-hip and skinny jeans that are too tight on the bottom half of your legs.	• For tighter styles, try going a size up and tailoring them. • Dark washes are most slimming. • Opt for minimal hip details, avoiding pocket embroidery.
Short	A classic style that doesn't overwhelm your small frame and one with a natural waist.	Wide-leg jeans and low rises.	• Wear legs slightly long, and pair your jeans with heels. • Darker rinses can have an elongating look. • Skinny styles should also be long, not cropped.
Boyish	Low-rise, straight-leg styles with a fitted behind.	Flares cut for curvier shapes.	• Slouchy boyfriend styles with feminine shoes can be chic. • You can get away with bigger, more detailed belts. • Tuck in your shirt to add shape. • Skinny jeans can be flattering.
Tummy	Styles that sit slightly lower than your natural waist or higher waistbands with stretch that can cinch you in slightly.	Anything super-low-rise and anything that snaps or buttons right near your belly button.	• Stretch is your friend here; find fitted (but not tight) styles. • Mid-rise versions will cover up love handles. • Boot-cut styles with flare balance proportions.
Short Waist/ Long Legs	A lower rise and a longer hem length.	High-waist styles and details around the top.	• Belts should blend in by being slim and neutral. • Skinny jeans with longer, untucked tops camouflage your waist. • Boyfriend styles that sit on the hips are great weekend alternatives.

Shape	Look for	Avoid	Don't Forget
Long Waist/ Short Legs	Styles that hit near your natural waist with straight or slightly flared legs.	Hip-huggers, cropped cuts and anything overly baggy.	• Trouser jeans with a tucked-in blouse can whittle the waist. • Flared styles should be subtle in shape. • Wear jeans with a cropped jacket to shorten the torso.
Large Bottom	A dark, even wash with a slight flare and stretch.	Super-skinny jeans, high-waist styles and really wide legs.	• Try a slightly lower rise; it will allow room for the derrière. • A boot-cut style will balance out the body. • Avoid small back pockets, which will make the behind look bigger.
Flat Bottom	Stretch jeans with slim legs that hug your bottom and have back-pocket details and a low-slung yoke.	Stiff denim, high waists, loose cuts such as boyfriend styles, and classic straight-leg shapes.	• Heels give your rear a lift. • Details on back pockets enhance your rear.

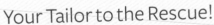

Your Tailor to the Rescue!

- Usually jeans come with enough extra material at the hem that a tailor can let them out and still reproduce seam details.

- If the flare is too dramatic, the inseam can be taken in from the knee down to eliminate some fullness.

- Some flared jeans can be transformed into straight-leg styles, and some straight-leg jeans can be pegged.

- Waistbands can be taken in, but pockets cannot be moved or removed, in part because of denim's fading properties—you'll be left with dark imprints where pockets once were.

how to wear it

Thanks to today's more casual approach to dressing, jeans are the backbone of many a wardrobe. With the right details, you'll make them work almost whenever you want.

Keep It Polished

There are still many places where jeans are not acceptable work attire, but if you're lucky enough to be able to wear them to work, the most sophisticated way is to pick a trouser cut in a dark rinse. Wear them with a jacket, a refined top or sweater, and heels or flats.

Add Some Color

Denim now comes in a rainbow of shades that can prove a fun alternative to basic blue. The best way to wear a colorful pair of jeans is to make them the standout piece in your ensemble. The rest of the outfit should be neutral and simple.

Make Your Jeans Your Own

Want to add some serious wear and tear to your favorite pair? First, bunch up random areas of your jeans and pour a bit of bleach on them. The bleached area will bleed out, so account for that. When your denim reaches the desired color, rinse well with cool water. Sand the fronts with heavy-grit sandpaper. Make cuts in the areas you want ripped, then pick apart the fabric's weave. Wash and dry your jeans twice for a killer distressed finale.

Dress Them Up

Jeans can quickly go from day to night if you choose a style with clean lines and minimal details. Pair sexy, white skinny jeans with a feminine top that has some panache. Dressy heels will also rachet up the wow factor.

denim q&a

You've got questions. We've got answers.

How do I know a pair of jeans is a good fit?

First, your jeans shouldn't dig into your flesh at the waist, and your backside should always remain covered—even when sitting in hip-huggers. Denim does give a little over time, but know the difference between a snug fit that will loosen and a fit that is just too tight. Inseam length is important. The average is 34 inches, but petites should go for 30 or 32 inches, and women over 5 foot 10 need 36 inches or longer. When it comes to fit at the thighs and the behind, it's so personal that the only rule of thumb is be wary of snug extremes—and visible panty lines.

Can I wear matching denim tops and bottoms?

If they are in the same rinse, wash and dye, then steer clear. If the shirt is soft and lightly faded, try contrasting it with a bottom that's structured and dark, such as a pair of skinny black denim trousers.

What about a jean jacket?

Great as an unexpected cover-up at night, the most interesting jean jackets are often cropped and body-conscious. Consider a size smaller than your regular coat (or scope one out in the boys' department). Push up sleeves to show jewelry. Make it your only denim element!

What finishes are best for work?

The old-school, plain, dark denim looks more polished than other blue finishes, and therefore is more office-appropriate. White denim in a trouser cut can also substitute for pants on casual Fridays.

How can I keep my denim dark?

Turn your jeans inside out before washing. Use only cold water, a light detergent and a thimbleful of vinegar, which works to set the color. Never put jeans in the dryer—lay them flat to dry instead.

How do I keep denim dye from staining my clothes and skin?

The trade-off with supersaturated indigo jeans is that the dye process for such a dark finish doesn't always set well. Before wearing dark jeans with light accessories or a light top, make sure they've been washed a few times. If smudging still occurs, take the stained item to a dry cleaner; special chemicals can be used to lift the dye without damaging your blouse, purse or shoes.

How should I wear a denim shirt?

Look for one that's feminine and fitted. If you want to do an oversize menswear version, belt it so your figure isn't lost, or pair with a mini or short shorts. If you wear it with jeans, do so with white or dark jeans only!

CHLOE SEVIGNY dresses down a flirty minidress by layering a fitted and distressed jean jacket on top. The jacket hits right at the waist, making her legs look extra long.

Low-cut, flared jeans in a light wash give EVA LONGORIA PARKER a casual vibe, but their perfect fit means they project polish. They are snug, but not too tight, and the long length adds height.

For a work-ready look, KATE WINSLET's dark-wash boot-cut jeans convey refinement, especially topped with a tailored jacket, simple heels and low-key jewelry.

VANESSA HUDGENS doesn't let her petite frame get swallowed up by a denim shirt. Instead, it's fitted to reveal her feminine silhouette, and with shorts (and slouchy boots), shows off her legs in a casual but edgy way.

the classic:
BOOT-CUT JEANS

Originally designed for farmers and workmen in the late 1800s and manufactured by Levi Strauss, jeans have evolved into a must-have staple for nearly all of us. Many styles enjoy popularity, perhaps none more than the boot-cut.

1: The rise (the material that extends from mid-waist through the crotch) should always fit comfortably without binding. If the rise hangs too low, it may make your legs seem shorter.

2: Your jeans should never be so tight that you can't put your hands in your pockets. If you can see the outline of the front pockets through your jeans, they are too tight.

3: Lightweight denim (less than 12 ounces) will reveal bulges. Instead, opt for more substantial weights—between 12 and 14 ounces. Heavier weights are less likely to wrinkle easily.

4: Unless you're wearing a tapered style (such as cigarette, capri or skinny), jeans should always fall so that there is a slight break where the hemline hits the top of your shoe.

1........

2...........

..........3

4

SKIRTS

chapter 8

For those times when you want to feel feminine in an instant, there's no better solution than to pull on a skirt and a pair of heels or pretty flats. You can look sharp and sexy in a pencil cut, fun in a mini, or simply elegant in a fuller, pleated version. No matter your mood, there's a skirt style to complement it. Best of all, you don't need a special occasion to wear a skirt—even if you're just running to the grocery store, your favorite flirty wardrobe item lets you flash a little skin in a flattering, sophisticated manner.

A black mini is anything but basic on the always fashion-forward KATE HUDSON. A diaphanous white blouse contrasts nicely with the panel-detailed skirt.

KERRY WASHINGTON's full, tiered skirt plays up her curves, while the slim-fitting blouse and long necklaces add balance with lean lines. Black pumps are a classic touch.

RACHEL BILSON goes for full-on feminine, pairing her lace-detailed skirt with a sweet, blush-colored cardigan. Strappy neutral sandals add length to her legs.

A pencil skirt becomes art when embellished with beads and shimmery details. ANGIE HARMON lets this stunning item do all the talking by keeping her shoes and top simple.

skirt style primer

While most women can wear many skirt shapes, one or two styles will quickly become your standout signature pieces.

Pencil

A pencil skirt can sit high, at or below the waist, and is fitted to the knees. Because it hugs your curves, it exudes sexiness.

A-Line

With a slight flare that runs from the waist to the knees, an A-line skirt is an elegant (and flaw-hiding) alternative to the body-conscious pencil.

Tiered

This skirt has layers or all-around ruffles that give it a soft, feminine shape.

Bubble

A bubble skirt widens in the middle, then tapers at the hem, usually at or above the knee, giving it a dramatic, poufed silhouette.

Mini

Full or slim, a mini is a carefree style that can go from day to night. (A desire to show off your legs is required!)

Full

With pleating, tucks or draping, a full skirt is a romantic choice that is flattering for most women. Pleats that fall from the hip are easier to wear than those that start at the waist.

skirts: flatter your figure

This feminine staple should both show off your legs and highlight your physique.

Shape	Look for	Avoid	Don't Forget
Curvy	Pencil skirts that don't hug the body too tightly and A-lines that fit gently over the hips.	Anything overly tight and full skirts that have too much pleating or draping at the waist.	• If you have a tummy, choose drop-waist styles. • Tuck in your shirt or use a belt to highlight your waist. • Your best length hits right at the knee.
Short	Pencil skirts, minis and narrow (as opposed to very full) A-lines.	Midcalf lengths and anything too full or girlish (especially if you are petite).	• Your hemline is important: It should hover above or just below the knee. • If you've got the legs, slim minis will give you length. • The flatter the shoe style you're wearing, the higher your hemline should be.
Boyish	Almost any style: You're lucky!	Anything too full if your shoulders are broad.	• If your hips are narrow, pleating can be flattering. • Slanted or patch pockets add definition to slim hips. • Show off your waist with belts and thicker waistbands.
Tummy	Lightly tapered pencil skirts and A-line styles with at-the-knee hemlines.	Pleats (even at the hip), wrap styles, front pockets and thick waistbands.	• Look for styles without a waistband or for slightly dropped waists. • Go for skirts with a simple, flat front or side zip. • Choose dark colors and matte textures. • Add brightly colored shoes to draw the eye down.
Short Waist/ Long Legs	A straight drop-waist shape that hits above your knee.	Wide waistbands, high-waist styles and other prominent details at the top of the skirt.	• Try back-zip styles that don't have a waistband and that sit on your hips. • A longer top with a slim mini is a good combination. • Hem details can draw the eye away from the waist. • You're better off without a belt.

Shape	Look for	Avoid	Don't Forget
Long Waist/ Short Legs	Something slim and straight that hits mid-thigh to right above the knee.	Full, pleated skirts and drop-waist styles.	• Pair skirts with a short jacket or top to break up a long line. • Use an off-center or front slit to make legs appear longer. • Try vertical details, such as subtle draping or seams.
Large Bottom	A moderate A-line, an easy wrap or a softly draped style.	Front pockets with details, styles with pleating all around, hem details and severely tapered shapes.	• Opt for styles without a waistband. • Choose mostly dark and muted colors. • Look for vertical details (such as a center pleat or stitching) to elongate your silhouette.

Your Tailor to the Rescue!

• Hems and side seams can be taken up or let out (just make sure hemlines can be steamed out). How much a hem can be altered depends on the amount of fabric available.

• If you are shortening a straight skirt, you should talk to the tailor about having it tapered to make sure the proportions remain the same. Most straight skirts can't be tapered any more than 2 inches without compromising your ability to walk.

• Skirts can only be widened if there is enough material.

• Waistbands can be removed or let out.

• Linings can be added or repaired, and some pleats and gathers can be removed. Closures can be replaced.

how to wear it

A good rule: The fit of your top should be the opposite of the fit of the skirt. A reliable length for most is between the top of the kneecap and about an inch below.

Va-va-va-voom Vibe

Skirts with prints, pleats, lots of draping or flourish should be paired with a clean, no-frills top. Also, if there's a lot of color on the skirt, go for a blouse in a neutral shade.

Weekend Play

A full miniskirt isn't constricting, and when paired with an untucked button-down shirt (especially layered with a fitted vest), looks casual but pulled together. Choose accents that give attitude.

Which Shoes Go with What?

Minis Go flat (ballet style) or go tall (strappy sandals, heels, pumps or ankle boots), nothing in between. Steer clear of kitten heels.

Full To make legs look long and lean, go for heels that match your skin tone.

A-Line/Pencil Narrower skirts look best with heels anywhere from 1 to 4 inches in height. Try pumps, slingbacks and peep-toes for work and strappy sandals for night.

Evening Elegance

Full skirts should be paired with something fitted. Stick with swingy materials that move with your body (lightweight cotton, chiffon, satin). Use accessories to play up the skirt's color.

TOPS

chapter 9

A top is like the exclamation point for any separates ensemble. The right style enhances your look by camouflaging problematic features (like a tummy and love handles) and showcasing your assets (such as toned arms).

Your closet should have several tops in a wide array of styles, including everyday button-fronts, weekend T-shirts and your sexier blouses. Invest in several good basics—a silk blouse that takes you from work to evening, for example. Otherwise, think of your tops as you would accessories: They're a fun opportunity to play with trends and, if desired, express your edgier, more provocative side. Try topping that.

A column of ruffles creates length and adds a feminine accent to EMILY DESCHANEL's outfit, especially tucked into her full skirt. The blush color complements her fair skin.

Horizontal stripes aren't for everyone, but MARIAH CAREY shows how they can flatter when limited to just a tank top and paired with a leg-lengthening mini and opaque tights.

Hooray for the basic white button-front! ALI LARTER demonstrates its timeless appeal when worn with equally crisp dark jeans and graphic peekaboo pumps.

A black beaded tank reveals JULIANNE MOORE's toned arms and, when paired with black pants, creates a lean, long silhouette. Her auburn hair is the perfect pop of color.

top style primer

Sexy, fun, whimsical or subtle, tops are a basic wardrobe necessity that is anything but boring. For those who like having endless options, nothing beats this clothing category.

Button-Front

Similar to a man's but with darts and seams to follow a woman's shape, it works with everything from pencil skirts to jeans.

Cap-Sleeve

This style has short sleeves that cover only your shoulders and the top part of your arms.

Wrap

A long, short or sleeveless top, it crisscrosses the body and ties at the waist.

Ruffled
Usually long-sleeve and made of silk or sheer cotton, it features a cascade of ruffles down the front.

Sleeveless
Whether it has a button-front or a zip-up back or details such as pleats and ruffles, a sleeveless blouse can highlight great arms and is a slim option to wear under a jacket.

Peasant
With a gathered or round neckline and blouson sleeves, this romantic silhouette softens any look.

t-shirt style primer

Nowadays, T-shirts—with their innovative materials and embellishments—can cost you a bit. Make sure you spend on styles that will pay you back in compliments.

Scoopneck

A scoopneck is generally flattering for most women. Wide scoops are good for narrow shoulders and large busts. Deeper scoops are good for slim and small-busted women.

Crewneck

This high, round style is usually fitted through the body on women's versions and is best for someone with a slim shape. It is not good for minimizing large busts or tummies.

Boatneck

The horizontal collar on a boatneck makes narrow shoulders appear broader and balances out wider hips and derrières.

V-Neck

This is a universally flattering neckline. The deeper the diagonal of the V-neck, the more slimming its effect. A wider V-neck can flatter women with narrow shoulders. Deeper Vs flatter a small or a large bust.

tank top style primer

If you're happy with your arms and want to flaunt them (and have a small- to medium-size bust), a tank top can be your alternative to a T-shirt or blouse.

Basic

A tank with a relatively high scoop neck and narrow but not spaghetti-style straps is good as a layering piece under jackets, cardigans and other looser or more revealing tanks.

Racerback

With straps that meet in the middle of the back, a racerback tank can be fitted or full. A normal bra won't work, so either invest in a racerback bra or layer another tank underneath it to cover any telltale straps.

Ornamented

Great for summer nights, an evening tank can come in luxe chiffon or satin and be embellished with beads, embroidery, pleats or ruffles. Try it under a jacket, with a cardigan or solo.

Empire

Romantic and easy to pair with slim skirts and pants, it's also the ultimate tummy concealer. The Empire cut gathers underneath the bust, below which fabric flows outward.

tops: flatter your figure

There's no shortage of shirt styles, but these tips are sure to help you narrow the field.

Shape	Look for	Avoid	Don't Forget
Curvy	Semifitted styles with seams and darts that end below the waist and that can be worn out or tucked in.	High, covered-up or buttoned-up necklines; you want to show a little skin for balance.	• Try flattering wrap styles. • Deep V-necks, small collars or narrow lapels look good. • Keep flourishes to a minimum. • Tops with a natural shoulder line will make you look leaner.
Short	Simple, fitted styles that are cinched around your natural waistline, not below it.	Anything too blousonlike, with an oversize print. Also, horizontal stripes.	• Opt for a slim fit at the shoulder. • Tops and bottoms in matching tones are elongating.
Boyish	Fitted shirts with seams and details that high-light your figure, such as shrunken men's-style shirts, cap-sleeve styles and slim V-necks.	Dolman- or kimono-sleeve tops and other voluminous cuts.	• You can enhance the bust with breast pockets and gathers. • Use wide collars to add shape to your silhouette. • Try halter tops.
Narrow Shoulders	Cap-sleeve styles or sleeves with accents such as pleats, gathers and minimal padding at the shoulder.	Sleeveless shirts that curve in at the shoulder and any top with a tight, narrow shoulder and sleeve.	• Peasant blouses can soften the shoulder line. • Breast pockets and wider V-neck openings create the illusion of breadth. • Prints should be large. • Horizontal stripes make you look broader.
Broad Shoulders	Sleeves with seams above the shoulders that aren't snug and don't have super-tailored armholes.	Wrap styles, wide collars and any kind of shoulder detail, such as pleats, padding or cuffed sleeves.	• Choose deep, narrow V-neck tops. • Keep collars and lapels narrow too. • A sleeveless shell can be flattering. • Avoid large prints; simpler is better.

Shape	Look for	Avoid	Don't Forget
Full Bust	Tops that are fitted but not too tight and that hit below the waist, as well as deep, vertical V-necks.	Anything too covered up at the top, anything cropped, and large prints.	• Keep the sleeve details simple. • Remember that a natural shoulder line gives a leaner appearance. • Styles with bust darts often fit better. • Scoop-neck T-shirts are flattering.
Small Bust	Fitted tops with breast pockets, gathers, ruffles, shirring or ruching near or over the bustline.	Voluminous shapes and dolman or kimono sleeves.	• Wear a top that's a brighter color than the bottom. • Try wide lapels and collars. • T-shirts with V-necks or low-scoop necklines are attractive.
Heavy Arms	Long or three-quarter sleeves and tops with slight pleating or tucking at the shoulder.	Sleeveless and strapless styles, and anything with sleeves that are too tight.	• Use long sleeves that flare below the elbow to balance arms. • Details at the collar and neckline draw the eye away from arms. • A peasant blouse or tunic can work if it is narrow at the torso.

Your Tailor to the Rescue!

- Collars can be made smaller and their points reshaped. A plain collar can be turned into a button-down.

- Buttonholes can be enlarged if you want to change buttons.

- Darts can be added to make a shirt fit better at the waist and bust.

- A shirt can be shortened (this is a good idea if there is too much fabric to easily tuck in the shirt).

- Sleeves can be shortened or tapered, and cuffs can be tightened or loosened.

how to wear it

Next time you reach for a shirt, consider the many ways you can easily add some extra oomph to your outfit with these ideas.

A Good Foundation

A plain T-shirt lets an ornate skirt or jacket take center stage. If you choose a colored shirt, be sure to keep other pieces in complementary hues or neutrals.

The Right Accessories

Tops that have a strong personality should be allowed to steal the spotlight. Earrings or bracelets are your best bet for jewelry when you've got an embellished or printed top.

Slimming Secrets

Worried about looking big in a blouse that adds volume to your frame? Instead of covering up, show a little skin. It might sound counterintuitive, but exposing your arms or décolletage flatters when it comes to blouson styles. Choose cuts with V-necks or button-fronts that open at the collar. Worn up to the neck, peasant-style shapes will make you look heavier. Wear them pulled down a bit instead to reveal shoulders.

Ladylike Luxe

When belted with a shiny ribbon, this ruffled sleeveless top looks black-tie ready even though it's untucked. Leaving a shirt untucked works best if it is wrinkle-free and neither too long nor too short; rather, it should hit right at the hip.

the classic:
WHITE SHIRT

A white button-front shirt might be the most basic menswear staple, but on a woman it becomes fresh and sexy. If this top received a report card, it would read, "Plays well with others." You can dress it up or dress it down, and it never goes out of style.

1: Choose a fabric such as cotton or twill with just the slightest bit of stretch. This will give the shirt some structure and eliminate any worry about the fabric being too sheer.

2: The body of the shirt should follow your contours without pulling or tugging across the back, under the arms or at the waist. It shouldn't gape open at the bust.

3: A longer-length shirt is the most versatile style because you can either tuck it into pants or skirts or wear it untucked and cinched with a belt.

4: A shirt's long sleeves should hit just before the joint in your thumb closest to your wrist. Any longer, and they will be unattractively dragging in, say, your soup bowl.

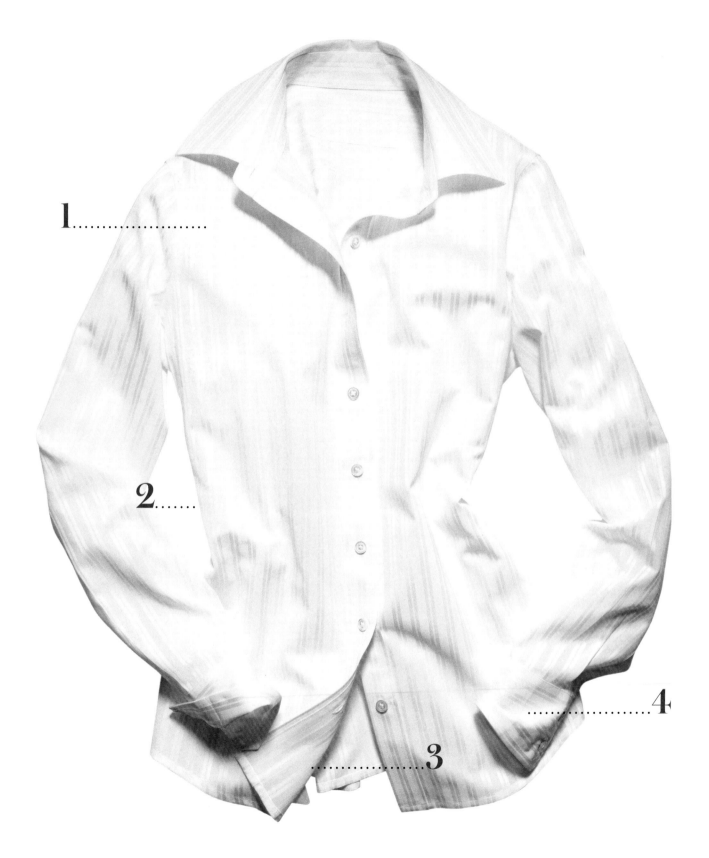

1....................

2......

3..................

4..................

chapter 10 SWEATERS

Whether it's your favorite summer-weight cotton cardigan worn to protect against that workplace AC or your thickest-knit cashmere turtleneck that keeps out the February chill, sweaters are a closet mainstay. They earn their safe place in our wardrobe because not only can they make us feel cozy, they're also multitaskers—they can accent a look or substitute for a jacket.

Some sweaters, such as those with metallic threads and/or embellishments, are the charismatic focal point of an outfit. Others, like a black cashmere crewneck or a gray cardigan, might not bring the same excitement, but they're fail-safe classics you rely on again and again. With that in mind, invest wisely in these core basics. Although a luxurious, well-made sweater can be costly, it's still better to buy one quality piece that looks great for years than to keep replacing a more affordable version that tends to pill or get stretched out beyond recognition (no warm and fuzzy feelings about that).

A sweater coat is all the heat HALLE BERRY needs to stay warm and look hot. The neutral beige hue complements her skin tone and lets her sexy LBD grab all the attention.

Bond vixen OLGA KURYLENKO shows off her slim physique in a thin-knit cardigan, which she fashionably layers over a pair of skinny jeans and metallic heels.

Keeping it basic and sophisticated with her neutral palette, ANGELINA JOLIE pairs narrow pants with a crewneck sweater that's loose but doesn't swallow her figure.

If a sweater isn't bulky, you can belt it, as HEATHER GRAHAM has with this sleeveless turtleneck. The wide belt complements the heavier weave of the sweater's knit.

sweater style primer

Sweaters are the ultimate layering piece, but that doesn't mean they can't be standouts on their own. These basic shapes also pile on a heavy dose of style.

Turtleneck
Whether it has a classic fold-over neck or a looser, draped cowl, this is the ultimate in warmth and generally flattering to all.

Crewneck
With its high, rounded neck, this knit is a reliable layering basic, especially when worn underneath a jacket.

V-Neck
From sexy, fitted, deep-V shapes to slightly looser menswear-inspired styles with banded hems and cuffs, a V-neck can be worn solo or with a blouse or T-shirt underneath.

Cardigan

This is a collarless button-down sweater in any number of knits (wool, cashmere, silk blend) that can feature a round neck or a V-neck.

Boyfriend

An oversize V-neck or cardigan style is a casual accompaniment to your weekend wardrobe.

Grandpa Cardigan

Thick or thin in weave, this cardigan features a shawl collar. More substantial versions can easily stand in for a jacket.

sweaters: flatter your figure

Work to find the right fit, and you'll probably have your go-to sweater for life.

Shape	Look for	Avoid	Don't Forget
Curvy	Wide V-neck pullovers and cardigans in a flat knit. Try adding a belt.	Anything very fitted, high crewnecks and turtlenecks with fitted fold-over necks. Chunky textures add bulk.	• A soft cowl neck or shawl collar that is not too bulky is flattering. • Styles with banded waistlines will only widen the midsection. • Opt for a self-belted cardigan.
Short	Fitted or semifitted sweaters that hit right below your natural waistline.	Any long boyfriend styles and shapes that are too full through the middle.	• Stick to turtlenecks with smaller necks; large cowls are overwhelming. • Choose a scoopneck with a slightly lower neckline and a hip-length hem. • A slim belt is best. • Steer clear of super-chunky weaves.
Boyish	Slim-fitting cardigans and pullovers that will flatter your trim shape; you can also get away with slouchy boyfriend styles.	Cardigans with sleeves that get wider instead of tapering and anything with an A-line.	• A boyfriend sweater should have long and slim proportions. • Turtlenecks should hit mid-hip or be slightly longer. • A body-hugging scoopneck can work with your shape.
Narrow Shoulders	V-necks with wide openings and embellishments. Boatnecks are a flattering option.	Crewnecks and turtlenecks in body-hugging knits that fit snugly at the shoulders.	• A cardigan with gathered shoulders looks good. • Chunky knits can add some padding to the shoulder area.
Broad Shoulders	Fine-gauge knits and soft, not super-fitted, shoulders.	Wide V-necks and bulky knits.	• A low-scoop neck can flatter. • A deep V-neck paired with a collared button-front shirt is slimming. • Avoid waistless and cropped shapes, as they will make you look boxy.

Shape	Look for	Avoid	Don't Forget
Full Bust	Scoopnecks and shallow V-neck pullovers and cardigans that show a bit of skin.	A crewneck or turtleneck that covers up too much.	• Try a soft cowl neck that shows just a hint of décolletage. • Softly shaped self-belted cardigans can flatter. • Choose styles that hit mid-hip for lengthening.
Small Bust	Fitted and semifitted shapes that follow your silhouette but don't hug too tightly.	Anything too voluminous, such as A-line shapes and full sleeves.	• Relaxed boyfriend shapes work as long as they are narrow. • Add a belt for waist definition. • Layer a shirt underneath. • Look for wide collars and cowl necks. • Chunky knits add balance.
Heavy Arms	Styles with wider, three-quarter sleeves that are soft in shape at the shoulder.	Skinny rib-knits and other curve-hugging weaves.	• Try shawl collars and cowl necks for balance. • Embellishments at the neckline draw the eye there. • If the sleeves are full, be sure the torso is long and lean.

Reweaving to the Rescue!

• There are two types of reweaves: the piece weave and the single-thread weave. In a piece weave, the weaver cuts a patch of fabric from an unnoticeable place, then weaves the patch into the fabric. The single-thread weave uses threads from the garment to reconstruct fabric.

• Stains, burns and iron marks are usually fixable. Large holes can be mended if there is enough material in the seams.

• Moth holes can be difficult to repair because they weaken surrounding fabric, so when you attempt to fix the hole, another spot often tears. Cashmere and wool are the most receptive to reweaving.

how to wear it

Sweaters are multitaskers that can be your best layering element, take the place of a top, or even stand in for a jacket or lightweight coat.

Long and Lean

For a slimming silhouette that also adds height, consider a thin-knit cardigan that hits below the hip. Vertical piping running down the center of the sweater will also make you appear more narrow and elongated through the torso.

Classic Casual

A long, striped fisherman-style sweater over narrow jeans is a tried-and-true weekend favorite. When layering, make sure the innermost piece is both lightweight and snug.

The Basics of Layering

A V-neck sweater looks sharp paired with a button-front shirt, but the shirt needs a defined collar to provide visual balance. A crewneck or a thin-knit turtleneck are great under blazers, and a cardigan can go over everything from a button-front shirt to a dress, tank top or T-shirt. Cashmere and cotton make ideal breathable-fabric choices for layering.

Top It Off

When worn in lieu of a coat, certain sweaters (especially those with embellishments or dramatic shapes) can easily be the star of your evening look. Go for contrasting textures underneath: Couple a sweater in an interesting weave with a silk dress accented by a beaded neckline.

the classic:
CASHMERE SWEATER

Cashmere wool comes from the downy underbellies of cashmere goats, which are usually raised in China and Mongolia. Because cashmere sweaters come in a variety of weights, this material works in your wardrobe year-round (and it doesn't itch!).

1: The highest-quality cashmere sweater has a linked collar. This means the collar is sewn into, not onto, the sweater. Also, any seams should lie flat and never visibly pucker.

2: Some cashmere is woven with wool or silk. These blends give the fabric a different texture and weight but still convey luxury. For an all-cashmere sweater, the denser the weave, the better.

3: Generally, the fuzzier the surface of the cashmere, the more pilling you can expect. Most sweaters will pill, especially if worn under another item. Almost all will pill at least a little under the arms.

4: Tight buttonholes are another sign of quality workmanship. Plus, they help the sweater retain its original shape longer. For the best fit, ribbed hems and cuffs should be smooth, not bulky.

LINGERIE

chapter 11

& *Shapewear*

Lingerie serves two very important but totally different roles in your wardrobe. First, the right undergarments can lift, hold in, smooth out and enhance your body's natural attributes. And second, lingerie can make you feel prettier, sexier and more feminine—and it's always worth remembering that when you feel good, you look good too.

Everyday bras and panties are an obvious must, but you also need a core group of problem-solving pieces, such as seamless underwear and other shapewear. They're your wardrobe's secret weapons, the unseen items that let you pull on your slinky or low-cut dresses with total confidence. Of course, you deserve to own a few fun "little nothings" as well, perhaps to wear with little (or nothing) else.

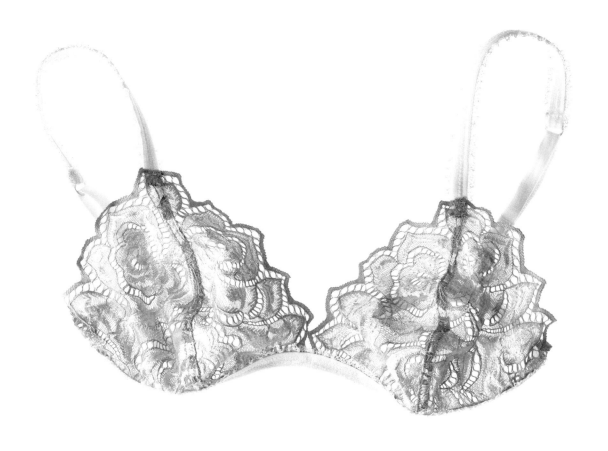

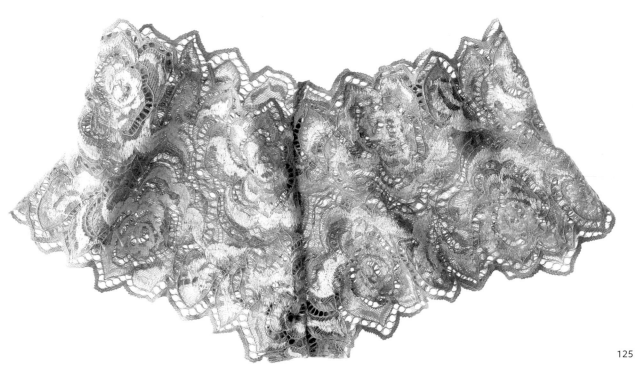

bra style primer

Most mornings your outfit will call for a modest, practical bra, and there are several shapes you should always keep at the ready. Consider these day-in, day-out styles.

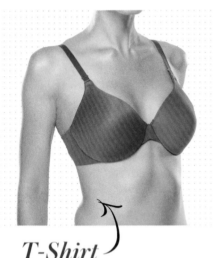

T-Shirt
A bra with molded or contour cups, it creates a smooth finish under even the lightest of tops.

Soft-Cup
A bra without structure, underwire, padding or molded cups, the soft-cup is very comfortable but offers minimal support.

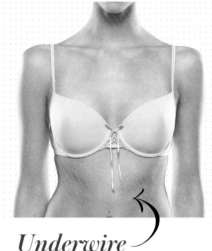

Underwire
This bra has flexible (metal or plastic) wire sewn under the bottom of cups to lift, separate and support breasts.

Push-Up
Padding can be in different places (along the sides, underneath or all over) to lift and/or push the breasts together.

Padded
This type of bra features either fiberfill, gel or air padding, which works to make the breasts appear larger.

Minimizer
A minimizer provides compression shaping, which allows large breasts to appear smaller under clothing.

specialty bras

For certain outfits, these four can make the look.

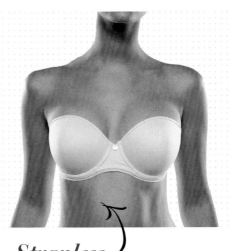

Strapless
This bandeau style has side bands and no straps. Versions are available both with and without underwires.

Plunging
For your low-cut numbers, this bra features a deep and wide V shape, and the band sits lower on the rib cage.

Halter
For dresses or tops of the same name, this style has one strap (sometimes removable) that fastens behind the neck.

Demi-Cup
A style that just covers the nipples and has wider-set straps, this model leaves the upper half of the breasts fully exposed.

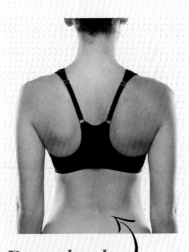

Racerback
A style with straps that make an X shape between shoulder blades, a racerback fits well under sleeveless or tank tops.

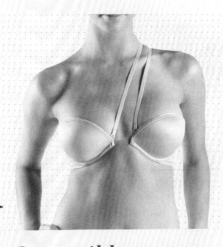

Convertible
Removable straps can be worn in different ways: as a halter, crisscrossed at the back, over one shoulder or strapless.

bra basics

Master these tips, and your days of wayward straps and constant adjusting will be history.

Find Your Size

A bra that fits you well will work harder than anything else in your wardrobe. Because the size, shape and firmness of your breasts change over time, what worked perfectly 10 years ago might not be right for you today. Seek out a bra-fit expert at a lingerie boutique or department store for expert help in determining your exact size and which styles best fit your shape. Or, grab a tape measure and do it yourself.

Here's How:

While wearing an unpadded bra—or no bra at all—wrap a soft tape measure snugly around your rib cage, just under your bust. Add five to the measurement (if the number is even, add six), and you've got your band size (32, 34, etc.).

Next, take a loose measurement across the fullest part of your bust.

The difference between the two measurements is your cup size:

    1 inch = A
    2 inches = B
    3 inches = C
    4 inches = D
    5 inches = DD
    6 inches = DDD

Remember: Bra sizing is not standardized (and European sizes are different from American sizes). What one maker calls a C cup could qualify as a B cup to another. All of this makes it important to remain open-minded when it comes to trying on different styles—in a range of sizes.

A Bra's Life Span

Your go-to, everyday bras usually last about a year. Preserve them by hand-washing using cold water and a gentle cleanser. Let them soak up to an hour, then hang to dry. If you do put your bras into the washing machine, use a lingerie bag, select the most gentle cycle with cold water, and avoid machine drying, which can damage the elastic or Lycra content of the bra and sometimes causes the underwire to pop out from its casing. If the elastic is worn or the straps are stretched, you need a new bra. (Also toss them if padding becomes lumpy, or straps or seams start to fray.) Good storage is crucial too: Lay molded-cup bras flat and stack them; fold all others, keeping them in neat piles. This maintains their shape and prevents tangling.

Strap

Two fingers should fit snugly side by side under the strap at the top of the shoulder, but it should still be taut enough that it won't shift around.

Bra Glossary

Cookies These are removable padded inserts—made of fiberfill or filled with water, oil or gel—that are used to change the shape of the breasts in the same way push-up bras do.

Contour Cup Made with a fiberfill or foam lining to eliminate nipple show-through and create a rounder shape.

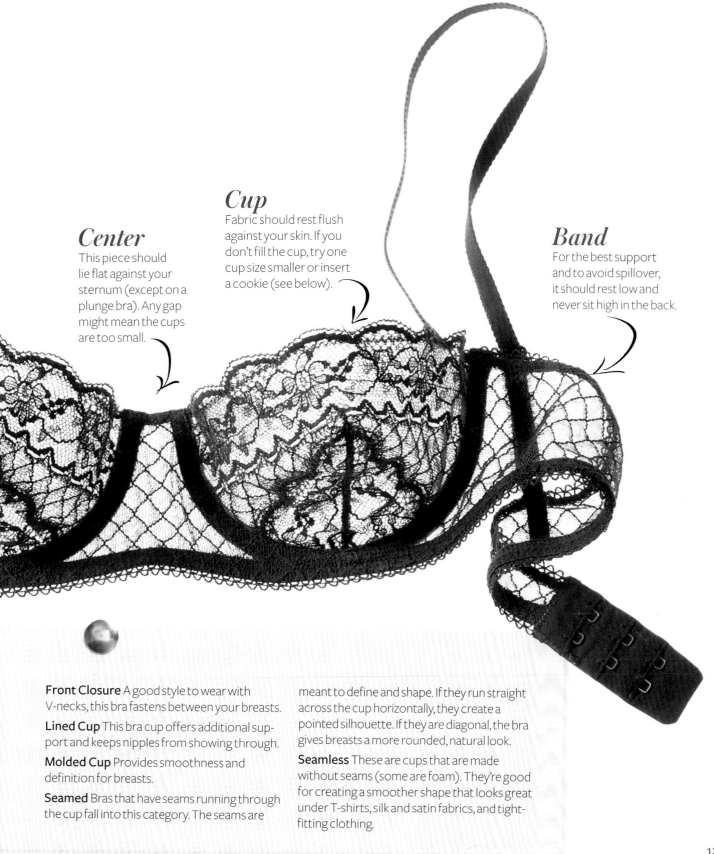

Center
This piece should lie flat against your sternum (except on a plunge bra). Any gap might mean the cups are too small.

Cup
Fabric should rest flush against your skin. If you don't fill the cup, try one cup size smaller or insert a cookie (see below).

Band
For the best support and to avoid spillover, it should rest low and never sit high in the back.

Front Closure A good style to wear with V-necks, this bra fastens between your breasts.

Lined Cup This bra cup offers additional support and keeps nipples from showing through.

Molded Cup Provides smoothness and definition for breasts.

Seamed Bras that have seams running through the cup fall into this category. The seams are meant to define and shape. If they run straight across the cup horizontally, they create a pointed silhouette. If they are diagonal, the bra gives breasts a more rounded, natural look.

Seamless These are cups that are made without seams (some are foam). They're good for creating a smoother shape that looks great under T-shirts, silk and satin fabrics, and tight-fitting clothing.

underwear styles

Without question, this is the garment you'll buy most often throughout the course of your life. There are four basic shapes, each with its own allure.

Bikini

Thin but not stringlike, the bikini's waistband rests below the navel and on the hips. It can also come in a string-bikini style, which has very narrow strips of fabric in place of side panels.

Boy Shorts

This is a low-rise style that extends to the top of the thighs, with full back coverage. The cut is good to wear under low-slung pants and skirts. A variation is tap shorts, which are loose from the waist and flare at the leg openings.

Brief

The waistband rests at or just below the navel, and back coverage is full. The legs may or may not be high-cut. (A high-cut brief is also known as French-cut.) This style is your best bet under short skirts and dresses. A control brief has added support to flatten the tummy or behind.

Thong

This style leaves the derrière mostly exposed in order to prevent the dreaded VPL (visible panty lines). Its cousin is the G-string style, which has no back coverage and a stringlike waistband.

shapewear 101

When your outfit is formfitting, you need a little help smoothing bulges. Self-control is a snap thanks to these marvels of high-tech fabric and expert construction.

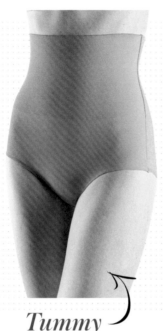

Bottom and Legs

A bike-shorts-style thigh tamer can banish saddlebag bulge, while a shorter version offers the same shaping when you're wearing a mini (some also lift the behind). A thin half-slip version can camouflage problem areas from your waist to your thighs.

Tummy

Nothing like the corsets and girdles of old, today's waist-cinchers are comfortable and work wonders. A high-waist brief can smooth out the stomach and hips. Other high-waist styles, such as capri or bike-shorts cuts, will create a lean line from the waist down.

Full Body

A slimming body slip might have a built-in push-up bra, or a three-quarter-sleeve underdress that keeps your arms and body looking toned. A leotard version with a built-in bra and stomach shaper keeps your torso in check, while a unitard style can make you look as if you've dropped a few pounds.

Top and Torso

A minimizing bodysuit reduces bust and waist size; a smoothing underwire style with adjustable straps can iron out any lumps; a slenderizing version supports the bust while whittling the waist; and a short-sleeve shaper helps eliminate underarm jiggle.

SHOES

chapter 12

We all have our particular weaknesses when it comes to footwear: Perhaps your closet is filled with pair upon pair of black boots? Red heels? Adorable flats? Slinky, strappy sandals? Hey, it happens. After all, shoes are the most seductive of accessories, and there are certain models (stilettos, anyone?) that can make us feel totally sexy, strong and wildly feminine. Then there are the more basic types of shoes. And while unadorned flat boots might not seem as exciting as bejeweled platforms, you'll probably wear the former far more often. With this in mind, be as choosy with your everyday shoes as you are with your standouts, and you'll always be walking tall.

shoe style primer

From sexy stiletto heels to sassy ankle boots, shapes and styles abound, just waiting to complete your look. Two dozen of the most popular models follow.

Pointy-Toes

Shoes with an exaggeratedly pointed toe, these can be either flats or heels.

Round-Toes

Shoes with rounded toes, these have fronts similar to those of ballet flats.

Pumps

Classic covered-toe, thin-heeled shoes, these can be a low, medium or high height.

Kitten Heels

These shoes can be slides or pumps. Their defining factor is a short heel (1 to 2 inches), which gives them a precious appeal.

Slingbacks

These are flat shoes or pumps that have a strap running behind the ankle to help keep the shoe secure on the foot.

Stilettos

Stilettos have thin, high heels that are usually at least 3 ½ inches in height.

Ballet Flats

Flat shoes with either no heel or the most minimal of heels, this style has a rounded toe reminiscent of ballet slippers.

Flats

Any shoes that have either no heel or a nominal one are considered flats.

Loafers

Slip-on shoes taken from menswear, these enclose the foot and have a high vamp (the top part of the shoe).

Oxfords

These lace-up, menswear-inspired shoes have low or high heels and details, such as punched-out designs in the leather.

Platforms

These high-heeled shoes have added height provided by extra-thick front soles.

Wedges

These shoes have a triangular-shaped heel that gives height while providing stability.

D'Orsays

These are shoes cut away at the sides, creating two sections—a toe and a heel portion.

Peep-Toes

With either flats or high heels, this style has a small opening at the front that allows a few toes to "peep" out.

T-Straps

A strap on these heels or flats comes up the top-center of the foot and attaches to a strap that goes around the ankle.

Sandals

These are any high, low or flat shoes that feature straps and do not cover the toes.

Strappy Sandals

Sandals, usually with stiletto heels, these have multiple straps crisscrossing in various patterns across the toes and ankles.

Slides

Open-toes with a high or low heel, slides are always completely backless. (Mules are similar, but with closed toes.)

Ankle Boots

Featuring either minimal or high heels, these boots cut off just below, right at or slightly above the top of the anklebone.

Flat Boots

Whether they are a knee-high equestrian style or a midcalf motorcycle shape, flat boots have low to nominal heels.

Tall Boots

Knee-high (or taller) boots, these can be slim and sexy or chunky and edgy.

Thongs

Distinguished by a strap that runs up between the big and second toes, this style includes flip-flops and sandals.

Espadrilles

Featuring flat or wedge heels traditionally of rope, these comfortable shoes can have closed or open toes.

Gladiators

These flat sandals, inspired by the versions once worn by Roman fighters, have many straps around the ankle and across the foot.

shoe flattery

The right shoes can perform small miracles for your entire look. These simple pointers will put you several steps ahead on the road to finding footwear that complements you from the ground up.

Pointy-toe heels elongate THANDIE NEWTON's legs.

Heel

A medium height (2 inches) flatters almost everyone. The most feminine type is slim, but the shape of the heel should match your body. For instance, skinny stilettos exaggerate the weight of a heavy frame, so thicker, stacked heels would be a better option.

Vamp and Throat

The vamp, or top part of the shoe, is the most slimming if cut low toward the toe in a V or U shape. High-vamp closed-throat shoes, when worn with skirts, can make legs look shorter. High-cut shoes look best with pants (skinny, for an edgy look), matching tights, or, if you dare (and are blessed with long, thin legs), miniskirts.

Toe

A tapered toe provides the slimmest look, but if you find pointy toes too uncomfortable, opt for oval shapes.

Straps

T-straps, ankle straps and wide straps over the instep will all draw attention to your feet. T-straps can elongate the legs if their color matches your skin tone; dark or embellished ankle straps usually shorten the appearance of legs.

Shoe Color

With evening wear it's OK for your shoes to match your outfit exactly. With black, you can have a little fun with colorful or even patterned shoes. Metallics work almost as a neutral and can be worn day or night. With lighter-colored outfits, black shoes can seem too heavy and make legs appear shorter. White shoes can be jarring and break up the silhouette of your leg, so opt for softer ivories or creams instead. A shoe that matches your skin tone will make your legs look longer.

Which Shoes Are Right for You?

Petite Too-high heels can make you look off-balance. If you're wearing flats, make sure they have a little lift. Match the tone of your shoes to your tights and skirt to elongate your legs.

Thick Ankles/Heavy Calves Wear the highest heels that you are comfortable in, but make sure they're not too spindly. Stacked heels or wedges are good options. Tall boots are also a smart choice. Midcalf boots often hit at the thickest part of the calf, so avoid these styles. Also, avoid square-toe styles, which may look too boxy.

HILARY SWANK matches her shoes to her jewel-toned evening dress to great effect.

high-heeled comfort

Even though high-heeled shoes can put seven times your body weight onto the balls of your feet, most women wouldn't dream of giving them up. Some ideas for finding the most comfortable pair.

Height and Stability

Low or kitten heels (1 to 2 inches high) are your most comfortable options. At any height, the thicker the heels, the more support and comfort they will give you. Spindly ones pitch you forward, causing you to balance all your weight on the balls of your feet.

Cushioning

Feel inside the shoes for padding. If padding isn't built in, invest in insert cushions (or ask a salesperson, since sometimes stores can provide cushions at no extra charge), but be sure the shoes still fit once you put them in. Your other option is to buy a pair in a larger size and wear it with full-foot orthotic inserts or gel pads.

Materials

Choose shoes made of soft, breathable natural materials, such as napa leather or goatskin. Synthetics can be eco-friendly (check up on the company and its claims), but they can make your feet sweat if plastic-based, and hard canvases will chafe. If your boots are stiff, wear them for one or two hours at a time with heavy socks until they are comfortable. Shop for shoes later in the day, when feet tend to be swollen. What feels good at 10 A.M. might feel tight at 4 P.M.

Alterations

There are a few things a cobbler can do to make your shoes more comfortable. Shoes made of leather can be stretched—including the bodies, straps and toe boxes. Extra cushioning can be added in the form of very thin rubber soles on the outside of the shoes or a pad inside beneath the insoles of most shoes, no matter their material. Some heels can also be lowered about 1/2 inch, depending on the shoe angle.

KATE MOSS is confident and elegant in comfortably high heels.

Stacked peep-toe heels on SIENNA MILLER both look sexy and provide stability.

Buying the Right Fit

Try different sizes. Not all size-8 shoes fit the same, even from one designer.

Walk on an uncarpeted surface. This is the only way to test how shoes will feel when pounding the pavement.

A shoe needs to feel like it fits but also look like it fits. "Shrimps" (toes dangling off the fronts of open-toe shoes) and "biscuits" (heels sliding off backless shoes) are deal-breakers.

Move. Wiggle your toes, flex your ankles, sit down and stand up. If any part feels tight or rubs, blisters are imminent.

Think ahead. Wear inserts or love thick socks? If so, bring them along, or buy a size that works with the extra material.

pairing shoes with clothes

Which shoes go with which looks? These matches were made in fashion heaven.

MISCHA BARTON pairs a minidress with satin flats for a mod evening look.

Peep-toe d'Orsay kitten heels flatter SELMA BLAIR's midcalf-length dress.

High Heels

For a daring statement, a short skirt with heels shows off your legs. Higher heels work with skinny, wide, boyfriend or distressed jeans, as well as flared or narrow pants. Stilettos make little black dresses and evening suits even sexier. For day, stacked and wedge heels are always appropriate.

Kitten Heels

These work with everything from knee- and midcalf-length cocktail dresses to office attire. A short skirt with heels shows off your legs, while a midcalf hemline works well with kitten heels.

Loafers and Oxfords

High-vamp slip-on, lace-up or tassled shoes, either as flats or heels, look perfect with pants of most lengths and widths. They also pair well with a pencil skirt and opaque tights.

Flats

These look best with narrow or cropped pants and jeans. If wearing flats with wide pants, pick a substantial style such as a loafer or brogue (a wingtip shoe). Flats also look elegant with short skirts—just know that you won't get the extra calf contouring provided by heels. Pointy-toe styles work well with long or short skirts as well as slim trousers, while ballet flats can work with cropped pants or, if your legs are thin, full skirts.

Boots

Knee-high flat boots look crisp with jeans tucked into them, under pants, and with slim knee-length skirts and minis. Midcalf boots are best under pants or worn with opaque tights and knee-length skirts. Ankle boots work with pants, short skirts and dresses. Think of high-heeled, knee-length boots as an alternative to pumps, to be worn with pants, skirts and knee-length dresses.

JOY BRYANT dresses up her boyfriend jeans with high-heeled boots.

hosiery 101

You'll get the greatest kick out of your hose or tights when you learn how to pair them with your shoes. The result? Legs that look lean and miles long.

Opaque tights create a long line from LUCY LIU's dress to her chunky sandals.

Black Opaque Hose

These flatter everyone and are often a necessity when the temperature dips. It's easiest to pair them with darker shoes, but they can be worn with contrasting colors.

Opaque Tights

You can wear opaque tights (black, brown, or other rich or vibrant hues) with dark shoes and certain open-toe shoes and sandals (but not with flat sandals). The thicker the straps on sandals, the easier it is to wear the shoes with tights.

Bright Tights

If you want a fun, bright shade on your legs, keep your shoes dark. We suggest not matching colored tights or hose to shoes exactly (red on red, for example), which makes for too much of a single hue in one area. Instead, choose shoes in the same color scheme but a slightly darker tone than what's on your legs.

Sheer Hose

Sheer black hose are dressier than opaque ones and work best worn with delicate shoes and most evening wear.

Nude Hose

These should disappear on your legs and not make them look yellow, gray or orange. Also, avoid darker shades that make your legs appear tan, especially when the rest of your body is not.

Textured Hose and Tights

Woven, lacy and knitted styles work best on thin or shapely legs. One exception: A sheer, fine vertical pattern can elongate legs.

Evening Shoes

Whether you want to go all out in a pair of sexy stilettos or would rather stick to something flat, now's the appropriate time to have some fun with extravagant details. Vibrant-colored satins, diamanté-encrusted appliqués, hardware, sequins, pearls—even feathers—are glam details that play well at night. Evening statement shoes work best with LBDs or streamlined gowns, but if you feel they overpower your outfit, opt for strappy sandals or d'Orsay pumps in metallic leather—always safe, timeless bets.

AMY ADAMS makes a statement on the red carpet in her ornate heels.

the classic:
STILETTO PUMPS

With the abundance of sexy shoes available, you might think high-heeled pumps would lose their allure. Hardly. After all, there are only so many places you can wear your favorite over-the-top shoes. But pumps? They're your eternally elegant footwear.

1: The top, back part of pumps should sit at a comfortable area on your heels and not constrict. The backs will move up and down slightly as you walk, and you don't want them to rub tightly and cause blisters.

2: For the most stability possible (and to keep your center of gravity in line with your spine and, therefore, the rest of your body balanced), the heels of shoes should be centered beneath your own heels.

3: Heels that are too spindly will require you to put all your weight on the balls of your feet. Look for heels that are slightly thicker at the top and taper to a thin tip (about $\frac{1}{2}$ inch wide is the standard).

4: A tapered toe gives feet the slimmest appearance. "Toe cleavage" is slang for the visible beginning of the crevice of your toes. Showing or flaunting toe cleavage is a personal preference.

1 ....

2 ....

3 ....

4 ....

BAGS

chapter 13

Your favorite handbag is a treasured accessory as well as a fashion workhorse: You take it with you wherever you go, use it to stash all of your essentials, and rely on it to pull together your outfit. Oftentimes your bag is first to telegraph your style to the world; you can be in a basic T-shirt and jeans, but with the right handbag, it's a look. There are fun, trendy bags, and then there are the classics, those pieces built for longevity. One of the latter can cost a pretty penny, but if it's made of fine leather and you take care of it properly, it will probably last longer than you could ever imagine—and might even become a cherished heirloom.

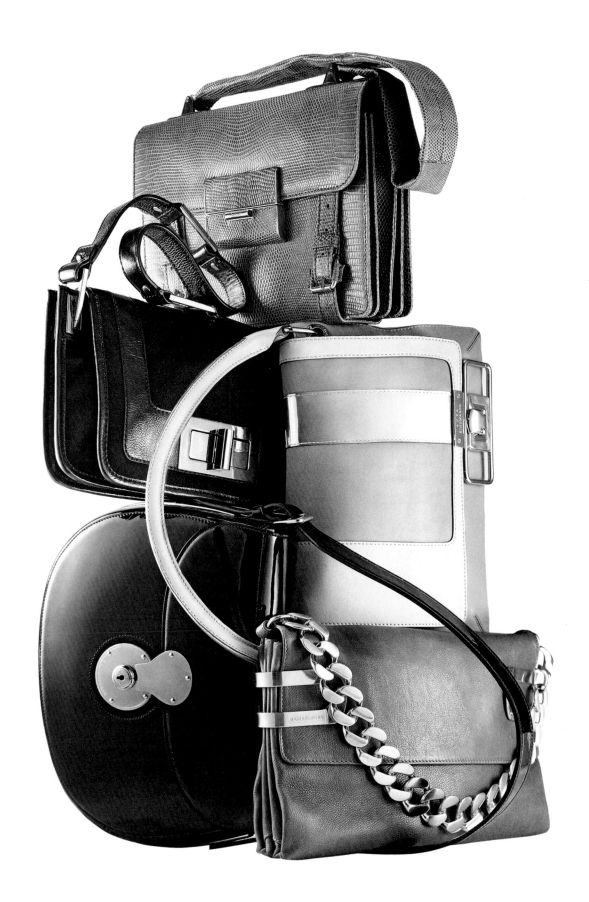

bag style primer

Changing your handbag is just about the fastest, easiest way to change your look—and there's a style for almost any statement you'd ever want to make.

Shoulder

This can refer to any bag that fits over the shoulder. Shoulder bags can have single or double straps.

Clutch

This is a small- to medium-size handheld bag.

Satchel

A leather bag with a rigid, flat bottom, it's usually rectangular with double straps.

Tote

A bag with short handles, it typically has an open top and is large enough to carry paperwork, a laptop or other larger objects.

Messenger

A small to medium-size rectangular bag, this style has a long, often adjustable strap that you can wear across your body, freeing up your arms.

Hobo

This bohemian-style bag is slouchy and has one strap that sits on the shoulder.

Evening

Beaded or crafted in rich materials, it can be a clutch style, or small and featuring thin straps, a long chain or a wristlet.

Structured/Ladylike

A bag with reinforced leather so that it holds its shape, it often has short straps that you either hold or dangle from your arm. Some also come with long chain straps to wear over the shoulder.

bag materials

Bags can be fashioned out of just about anything, from natural fabrics to man-made materials. Here, a roundup of your many options and what to expect from each.

Nylon

Nylon is a versatile, weather-repellent handbag fabric. Depending upon their composition, weave and attendant hardware, nylon bags run the gamut from inexpensive to high-end.

Leather

Better bags are made of leather, because it is a durable, breathable material. Good leather can last decades; cheap leather is usually papery and tears easily. Leathers with grain or pebble textures show the least wear.

Patent Leather

The leather of these bags has been coated with oils and dried so that its surface is super shiny.

Exotic Skins

Alligator tends to be the most expensive skin, followed by ostrich, lizard, python and snakeskin. Most exotic skins are desirable for their texture and durability, and can last decades with proper care and storage.

Hardware

Hardware can be decorative—with studs, grommets and designer ID tags—or functional, as in buckles, zippers and rings to hold straps. The best hardware is made from brass, which is plated with various metals to achieve gold, silver or copper finishes.

Canvas

Typically woven from cotton, linen or hemp, canvas is a casual, inexpensive material that can also be treated with polyurethane to give it shine.

Embellishments

Crystals, diamanté, semiprecious stones, sequins and embroidery can all be featured on bags, especially satin evening styles.

three must-have bags

You'll probably own many more, but these are reliable basics.

MOLLY SIMS's slouchy tan bag goes with lots of hues, including those in her red floral print dress.

FREIDA PINTO's clutch with hardware serves as a standout evening accessory.

Structured Day Bag

This is the bag you will use the most, not only because it is your home away from home, but also because it is the most versatile. It will look right with suits and dresses, and will add polish to casual looks, like jeans. Decide what size bag to get by considering how much you'll carry inside it. If your essentials are bulky, you'll want a bag with space, like a roomy, more-rigid satchel. If your needs are more spare, a smaller shoulder style works. Your go-to bag should be in a neutral shade such as black, rich brown, gold or tan; whites are crisp, but keep in mind that you'll need to maintain their look.

Casual

A casual bag, whether it is a slouchy hobo, an edgy messenger or a classic tote, should be determined by what you wear on your days off and, again, on how much room you need. There is no reason to choose something understated here. Opt for hardware details or shades that pop; it is a great way to add vibrancy and texture to your weekend wardrobe. Just make sure hardware doesn't weigh too much, or you'll strain your back when toting it around for long periods of time at the mall or flea market, or on other outings.

Evening

These bags fall into two categories: the great, go-with-everything classics and the fun, exotic little gems. A simple black, silver or gold metallic clutch usually works with both over-the-top gowns and LBDs. Otherwise, have fun. From deep-hued minaudières to Day-Glo-colored satin fold-overs, this is one category of accessory in which you should buy a piece that makes you swoon.

JESSICA BIEL steps out with a spacious white day bag with gold accents that conveys elegance.

buying the right bag

The perfect one should be comfortable to carry, keep you organized and make you look sharp. Below, key questions to ask yourself when making your next purchase.

1. How does it look?

Just because it is the most gorgeous thing you have ever seen on the shelf doesn't mean the bag will be perfect on you. Try it on like you would a dress—at a full-length mirror, scrutinizing every angle. The bag should be in proportion to your figure and size. Too large, and a bag is overwhelming. Too small, and it makes you look large by comparison.

2. How does it feel?

If you prefer a shoulder bag, be sure its strap is a width that sits comfortably on your shoulder. Walk around a bit and see if the strap slips. Does the bag sit nicely under your arm? Is it light enough? Test it out with all your usual accoutrements inside—wallet, phone, etc. If it's too heavy, it can strain a narrow strap, dig into your shoulder, or cause back and shoulder pain.

3. Will it keep me organized?

There are two ways to organize your bag: Choose one with interior and exterior pockets for you to stash your cell, wallet, keys and other items in, or buy zippered pouches to keep your items separated. In a medium-size or large day bag, you definitely want at least one or two pockets for everything, or you'll waste time digging around for your keys or cell phone. Also, be sure the bag is secure enough, with a zipper, button, embedded magnet, flap or drawstring closure. (You don't want your wallet falling out or an opening that's tempting for pickpockets.)

4. Does it fit my lifestyle?

Think about when and where you will use your bag. If you commute with periods of walking outdoors, sometimes in inclement weather (to the bus or train, or in an open parking lot to your building or home), an untreated white suede hobo is not going to be your best bet. Instead, opt for darker hues in durable materials, including treated leathers, canvas and nylon. Also, keep the weight of the purse in mind. Extra hardware and details can make for heavy lifting after a while. And if if you have children and need your hands free, a handheld bag could quickly become a nuisance.

Slouchy vs. Structured

When it comes to day bags, options abound, but if you need lots of room, we suggest a slouchy hobo or a structured ladylike handbag. These are two very distinct looks, so which one suits you best?

Slouchy Hobo These relaxed medium- to long-strap carry-alls are roomy enough to cart around all your gadgets, a book, planner, wallet, cosmetics case and sometimes a change of clothes—even another pair of shoes (hint: keep them wrapped in a bag to protect other items and the lining). These bags convey effortless style and look best with more casual outfits.

Structured Ladylike Handbag Sleek, chic and utterly feminine, this vintage-looking, medium- to short-handle frame bag often fits in the crook of your elbow or dangles from your wrist. It is a power statement (this is the Queen of England's choice, after all!) and projects both sophistication and polish. This bag elevates jeans and complements office looks.

the classic:
LADYLIKE BAG

Many women have an emotional attachment to their handbags, which is perfectly understandable: Not only is it equivalent to a portable office, but a beautiful carryall can also have a major style impact—instantly upgrading even the most basic outfit.

1: Whether it is croc-embossed, grainy, smooth or shiny, the leather your bag is made of should feel like leather—thick, durable and substantial. Cheap leather will fray or rip quickly.

2: Check the stitching of the bag. The size of the stitches should be even, and they should run in a straight line along the seams. The bag should also appear sturdy enough to hold some weight.

3: The best hardware is plated brass, which feels solid in your hand. Inferior metals are cheaper but often tinny or hollow. Check function too: Snaps should all close, and locks should turn with ease.

4: A good bag should always have a lining. Some are lined in leather, which is considered the most luxurious. Others are lined in either silk or cotton, which are also reliable options.

1........

2.....

3

4

CLOTHING & PHOTOGRAPHY
credits

Clothing Credits

p. 18, from left to right: look 1, cardigan: Hanii Y, T-shirt: Gap, pants: Elie Tahari, sunglasses: Target, watch: Michael Kors, necklace: Kendra Scott, sandals: Anya Hindmarch; look 2, top: Geren Ford, shorts: Loeffler Randall, necklace: Pono by Joan Goodman, handbag: Chanel, sandals: Calvin Klein

p. 19: camisole: Diesel, skirt: DKNY, earrings: Linda Levinson Designs, necklace: Vanessa Montiel, purse: Jamin Puech, sandals: Miu Miu

p. 26: wrap: Vivienne Tam, shift: Michael Kors, strapless: Calvin Klein

p. 27: sheath: Shoshanna, A-line: Nieves Lavi, empire: Vera Wang Lavender Label

p. 28: halter: Ralph Lauren Black Label, bias-cut: Hollywould, asymmetrical: Kenneth Cole

p. 29: shirtdress: BCBG Max Azria, full: Isaac Mizrahi for Target

p. 31: Badgley Mischka

pp. 32–33, from left to right: look 1, dress: House of Spy, top: 10 Feet, earrings: Pure Pearls, bag: Longchamp, shoes: Delman, watch: New York & Company, glasses: Leiber Eyewear; look 2, dress: M Missoni, earrings: Lynda K. Jewelry, clutch: Felix Ray, shoes: Jean-Michel Cazabat; look 3, dress: Elie Tahari, earrings: Marcia Moran, clutch: Kotur, pumps: Badgley Mischka, bangles: Skinny

p. 34: romantic: Abaeté, sophisticated: Vera Wang Lavender Label

p. 35: sexy: Black Halo, edgy: Twelve by Twelve

p. 38: tuxedo: Agnés B., menswear-tailored: Ralph Lauren Blue Label, peplum: Julie Haus

p. 39: boyfriend: Gap, military: Nicole Miller Collection, bomber: Express, safari: DKNY

p. 41: Milly

pp. 42–43, from left to right: look 1, blazer: Theory, dress: ECI New York, bracelets: By

Malene Birger, pumps: Guess by Marciano, cosmetics clutch: Dior; look 2, jacket: Sisley, top: J. Crew, earrings: Sparkles for Tres Jolie, tote: Kate Spade, pumps: Charles David, bracelet: Marine Rocks; look 3, jacket: Karen Walker, dress: Reiss, top: Sweetees, belt: Karen Walker, shoes: Colin Stuart for Victoria's Secret Catalogue, earrings: Silpada

p. 45: Luciano Barbera

p. 48: tailored: Rebecca Taylor, feminine: Strenesse Blue

p. 49: Theory

p. 51: Just Cavalli

pp. 52–53, from left to right: look 1, suit: Fashionista, purse: Anya Hindmarch, pumps: Bettye Muller, bangles: Ted Rossi, earrings: Hamilton Jewelers; look 2, jacket and skirt: Tory Burch, bracelet: DKNY, pumps: Bally, tote: Etienne Aigner, earrings: Mollybeads; look 3, blazer and pants: Venus, top: Rock & Republic, necklaces: Erickson Beamon, metal frames: Original

Penguin, briefcase clutch: Sigerson Morrison, heels: Cole Haan

p. 57: Sieze sur Vingt

p. 60: military: Sonia Rykiel, peacoat: APC, car: Milly

p. 61: cape: Charles Nolan, topcoat: H & M, wrap: Adrienne Vittadini

p. 62: parka: Moncler, trenchcoat: London Fog, cocoon: Gap

p. 63: toggle: United Colors of Benetton, chesterfield: Kors by Michael Kors, bracelet-sleeve: Forever 21

p. 65: Gryphon

pp. 66–67, from left to right: look 1, shirt: Brioni, coat: Foley + Corinna, bag: Alexis Hudson, shoes: Boss Black, cuff: Nashelle; look 2, coat: Alice + Olivia, dress: Marc by Marc Jacobs, earrings: Gold Label by Tina Tang, pumps: Botkier, clutch: Emporio Armani; look 3, coat: Vivienne Tam, necklace: Roxanne Assoulin for Lee Angel, earrings: Diamondair, shoes: Courtney Crawford, pants: Strenesse Gabriele Strehle, bracelet: Diamondair, clutch: Jane Bolinger

p. 71: Burberry

p. 74: pleated: Sisley, skinny: D&G, cropped: Walter

p. 75: high-waist: Badgley Mischka, boot-cut: Development, wide-leg: Chaiken

p. 77: J. Crew

pp. 78–79, from left to right: look 1, jacket: Sisley, camisole: J. Crew, belt: Metro 7, earrings: Erica Weiner, bracelets: Peruvian Connection, pumps: BCBGirls, pants: Chadwick's, bag: Adrienne Vittadini; look 2, cardigan: Bebe, top: Kelly Nishimoto, necklace: Jigsaw, bag: Longchamp, shoes: Michael Kors, pants: Isaac Mizrahi for Target, belt: Terry Stack, earrings: Diamondair; look 3, cardigan: Schumacher, shirt: Martin + Osa, watch: Badgley Mischka, leggings: Level 99, flats: Maloles, earrings: Julie Sandlau

p. 81: short shorts: Vera Wang Lavender Label, Bermudas: Elie Tahari

p. 84: straight-leg: DVB, trouser: Anlo, boot-cut: Raven Denim

p. 85: boyfriend: Current/Elliott, skinny: Levi's, high-waist: Genetic Denim

p. 87: J Brand

pp. 88–89, from left to right: look 1, turtleneck: Emma & Posh, jeans: Anne Leman, flats: Jimmy Choo, bangles: Hermès; look 2, anorak: Rag & Bone, tank: Rebecca Taylor, purse: Banana Republic, pants: AG Adriano Goldschmied, flats: Maloles; look 3, necklace: D&G, jacket: Theory, top: Roberta Freymann, jeans: Genetic Denim, heels: Christian Louboutin

p. 93: Fidelity

p. 96: pencil: Theory, A-line: Philosophy di Alberta Ferretti, tiered: Corey Lynn Calter

p. 97: bubble: Rebecca Taylor, mini: Walter, full: Topshop

p. 99: Theory

pp. 100–101, from left to right: look 1, necklace: Pono by Joan Goodman, top: Rebecca & Drew Manufacturing, belt: Jacqueline Jarrot, bag: Bulga, shoes: Melanie Dizon, skirt: Banana Republic, watch: BCBG Max Azria, jacket: Gerard Darel; look 2, hat and shirt: Original Penguin, vest: Express, clutch: Andrea Brueckner, boots: Cole Haan, frames and leather case: Selima for Jack Spade, chain: Wendy Nichol; look 3, necklace: Glam Rock, cardigan: J. Crew, reversible tank: Lafayette 148 New York, bracelet: Lia Sophia, skirt: Tracy Reese, clutch: Kotur, sandals: Michael Kors, earrings: Diamondair

p. 104: cap-sleeve: Banana Republic, button-front: Elizabeth and James, wrap: Ann Taylor Loft

p. 105: sleeveless: Banana Republic, ruffled: Badgley Mischka, peasant: Milly

p. 106: scoopneck: Dream Society, crewneck: American Apparel, boatneck: Joie, V-neck: Young, Fabulous & Broke

p. 107: basic: Theory, ornamented: Cecilia de Bucourt, racerback: Alexander Wang, empire: Elizabeth and James

p. 109: Rock & Republic

pp. 110–111, from left to right: look 1, shirt: Line, bag: Kenneth Cole, skirt: Rachel Roy, flats: Sigerson Morrison, jacket: Nili Lotan; look 2, blouse: Koppani, earrings: Lulu Frost, belt: Terry Stack, brooch (on belt): Tatty Devine, skirt: Ralph Lauren Black Label, clutch: Lambertson Truex, flats: Tibi, bracelets: Gerard Yosca; look 3, blouse: White House/Black Market, earrings and bracelet: Express, skirt: Ann Taylor, shoes: Aldo, clutch: Mundi

p. 113: Banana Republic

p. 116: crewneck: White + Warren, V-neck: Old Navy, turtleneck: Spanx

p. 117: boyfriend: Trovata, cardigan: Rebecca Taylor, grandpa cardigan: Theory

p. 119: United Colors of Benetton

pp. 120–121, from left to right: look 1, cardigan: Trina Turk, dress: J. Crew, belt: Sisley, wedges: Old Navy, bracelets: A.V. Max; look 2, sweater: Demylee, shirt: Michael Stars, earrings: Miriam Haskell, shades: Ray-Ban, jeans: Levi's, flats: Elie Tahari Collection, bag: MCM; look 3, sweater: Walter, dress: Mint Jodi Arnold, earrings: Kim Alessi, slingbacks: Delman

p. 123: Ann Taylor

p. 125: bra and boycut briefs: DKNY Underwear

p. 126: T-shirt: Bali, soft cup: Gap Body, underwire: Wacoal, minimizer: Bali, padded: Le Mystère, push-up: Huit

p. 127: strapless: Chantelle, plunging: Frederick's of Hollywood, halter: Dr. Rey's Shapewear, convertible: Victoria's Secret, racerback: Natori, demi-cup: Simone Pérèle

pp. 128–129: Eres

p. 130: bikini: Felina, boy shorts: Huit, brief: Jockey, thong: Gap Body

p. 131: bottom and legs: Grenier, tummy: Wacoal, full body: Wolford, top and torso: the Body Wrap

p. 133: Badgley Mischka

p. 134: pointy-toes: Kate Spade, round-toes: Kate Spade, pumps: Salvatore Ferragamo, stilettos: Jimmy Choo, slingbacks: Christian Louboutin, kitten heels: Giorgio Armani

p. 135: ballet flats: J. Crew, flats: Bettye Muller, loafers: Christian Louboutin, wedges: Guess, platforms: Christian Louboutin, oxfords: Benetton

p. 136: d'Orsays: Cynthia Vincent, peep-toes: Casadei, T-straps: Oscar de la Renta, slides: Steve Madden, strappy sandals: Ralph Lauren, sandals: Loeffler Randall

p. 137: ankle boots: Guess by Marciano, flat boots: Ralph Lauren Collection, tall boots: Carlos by Carlos Santana, gladiators: Jimmy Choo, espadrilles: Vera Wang Lavender Label, thongs: Madison Harding

p. 143: Christian Louboutin

p. 145, clockwise from top: Calvin Klein Collection, Anya Hindemarch, Michael Kors, Ralph Lauren Collection, Banana Republic

p. 146: shoulder: Balenciaga, clutch: Nancy Gonzalez, tote: Vivre, satchel: Retrodelic

p. 147: hobo: Jimmy Choo, messenger: Oliver Spencer, structured/ladylike: Yves Saint Laurent, evening: Steve Madden

p. 148: leather: Prada, nylon: Gap, patent leather: Michael Kors

p. 149: exotic skins: Borbonese, hardware: Miu Miu, embellishments: Escada, canvas: Tory Burch

p. 151: slouchy hobo: Salvatore Ferragamo, structured ladylike: Banana Republic

p. 153: Hermès

Photography Credits

p. 9, from left to right: Eugene Gologursky/WireImage, Arlene Richie/JPI, LAN/Retna, Splash

p. 10, from left to right: Glenn Weiner/Zuma Press, Jean-Paul Aussenard/WireImage

p. 11, from left to right: James Devaney/WireImage, Courtesy of Burberry

p. 14: Istock.com

p. 15, from left to right: AT1/Xposure/StarMax, Dave M. Benett/Getty

p. 16, from left to right: Clark Samuels/Startraks, Paul Fenton/Zuma Press, Gilbert Flores/Celebrity

p. 17, from left to right: Ethan Miller/Getty, Gilbert Flores/Celebrity, Retna

p. 18, from left to right: Brian Henn, Tony Barson/WireImage, Brian Henn

p. 19, from left to right: Rabbani and Solimene/WireImage, Brian Henn, Frazer Harrison/Getty

p. 20, from left to right: Steve Granitz/WireImage, Evan Agostini/WireImage

p. 21, from left to right: Jeffrey Mayer/WireImage, Richie Buxo/Splash, Evan Agostini/WireImage

p. 22: Jim Smeal/BEI

p. 23, from left to right: Vince Flores/Celebrity, Theo Wargo/WireImage, Bill Davila/Startraks

p. 25, from left to right: Bill Davila/Startraks, Sara Jaye Weiss/Startraks, Andreas Branch/Sipa, Bauer-Griffin

p. 26, from left to right: Grant Cornett, Manfred Koh, Brian Henn

p. 27, from left to right: Kevin Sweeney, Manfred Koh, Sabrina Grande

p. 28, from left to right: Dawn Giarrizzo, David Lawrence, Kevin Sweeney

p. 29, from left to right: Dawn Giarrizzo, Grant Cornett

p. 31: Manfred Koh

pp. 32–33: Sabrina Grande (3)

p. 34, from left to right: Time Inc. Digital Studio, Gilbert Flores/Celebrity, Kevin Sweeney, Scott Wintrow/Getty

p. 35, from left to right: Kevin Sweeney, Janet Mayer/Splash, Kevin Sweeney, Dave Allocca/Startraks

p. 37, from left to right: Billy Farrell/PMC/Sipa, Theo Wargo/WireImage, George Pimentel/WireImage, Albert Michael/Startraks

p. 38, from left to right: Don Penny, Dawn Giarrizzo, Kevin Sweeney

p. 39, clockwise from top left: Brian Henn, Virgil Bastos, Devon Jarvis, Grant Cornett

p. 41: David Cook

pp. 42–43, from left to right: Kevin Sweeney/Manfred Koh, Sabrina Grande (2)

p. 45: Devon Jarvis

p. 47, from left to right:
Emmi Vi/Flynet Pictures, Gilbert Flores/Celebrity, Jason LaVeris/FilmMagic, Mychele Daniau/AFP/Getty

p. 48, from left to right: Time Inc. Digital Studio, Brian Henn

p. 49: James Westman

p. 51: Sabrina Grande

pp. 52–53, from left to right: Sabrina Grande, Brian Henn/Don Penny, Sabrina Grande

p. 54: Lisa O'Connor/Zuma Press

p. 55, from left to right: Jill Johnson/JPI, Dave M. Benett/Getty, Mike Emory/BA/BEI

p. 57: Virgil Bastos

p. 59, from left to right: Jeff Vespa/WireImage, courtesy of Burberry Prorsum, Richard Young/Startraks, Pacific Coast News

p. 60, from left to right: Sabrina Grande, Kevin Sweeney, Brian Henn

p. 61, clockwise from left: Kevin Sweeney (2), Manfred Koh

p. 62, clockwise from top: Kevin Sweeney, Brian Henn, Sabrina Grande

p. 63, clockwise from left: Kevin Sweeney, Sabrina Grande, David Lawrence

p. 65: Kevin Sweeney

pp. 66–67: Sabrina Grande (3)

p. 68, from left to right: Dan Herrick/Zuma Press, Joseph Marzullo/Retna

p. 69, from left to right: Thos Robinson/Getty, James Devaney/WireImage

p. 71: Dawn Giarrizzo

p. 73, from left to right: Jennifer Graylock/JPI, Marc Susset-Lacroix/WireImage, INF/Goff/Dara Kushner, Brian Zak/Sipa

p. 74, from left to right: Manfred Koh (2), Brian Henn

p. 75, from left to right: Virgil Bastos (2), Dawn Giarrizzo

p. 77: Brian Henn

pp. 78–79: Sabrina Grande (3)

p. 80, from left to right: Ed Geller/Globe, Jennifer Buhl/Pacific Coast News

p. 81, clockwise from left: Frederick Breedon/WireImage, Dawn Giarrizzo, Kevin Sweeney, Freddy Baez/Startraks

p. 83, from left to right: Dakota/PIP, Todd Williamson/WireImage, Demis Maryannakis/Splash, Bill Davila/Startraks

p. 84, from left to right: Dawn Giarrizzo, David Lawrence, Dawn Giarrizzo

p. 85, from left to right: Brian L. Colby, David Lawrence, Dawn Giarrizzo

p. 87: Brian Henn

pp. 88–89, from left to right: Sabrina Grande, Brian Henn, Don Penny/Brian Henn

p. 90: Alexander Tamargo/WireImage

p. 91, from left to right: Sara De Boer/Retna, David Gadd/Globe, INF Photo/INFphoto.com

p. 93: Brian Henn

p. 95, from left to right: Gilbert Flores/Celebrity, Jamie McCarthy/WireImage, Fernando Allende/Celebrity, Donato Sardella/WireImage

p. 96, clockwise from left: Brian Henn, Dawn Giarrizzo, Grant Cornett

p. 97: Kevin Sweeney (3)

p. 99: Grant Cornett

pp. 100–101: Sabrina Grande (3)

p. 103, from left to right: Charles E. Shelman/FilmMagic, Marc Susset-Lacroix/WireImage, Dimitrios Kambouris/WireImage, Brad Barket/Getty

p. 104, clockwise from left: Alexander Milligan, Dawn Giarrizzo, Kevin Sweeney